UNIVERSITY CASEBOOK SERIES®

2018 SUPPLEMENT TO

CONSTITUTIONAL LAW

NINETEENTH EDITION

KATHLEEN M. SULLIVAN

Partner, Quinn Emanuel Urquhart & Sullivan, LLP
Former Professor of Law and Dean of the School of Law,
   Stanford University
Former Professor of Law, Harvard University

NOAH FELDMAN

Felix Frankfurter Professor of Law,
Harvard University

FOUNDATION
PRESS

University Casebook Series is a trademark registered in the U.S. Patent and Trademark Office.

© 2017 LEG, Inc. d/b/a West Academic
© 2018 LEG, Inc. d/b/a West Academic
    444 Cedar Street, Suite 700
    St. Paul, MN 55101
    1-877-888-1330

Printed in the United States of America

ISBN: 978-1-64020-875-9

TABLE OF CONTENTS

TABLE OF CASES..V

Chapter 1. The Supreme Court's Authority and Role.......................1
Section 4. Constitutional and Prudential Limits on Constitutional
    Adjudication: The "Case or Controversy" Requirements 1

**Chapter 3. The Commerce Power and Its Federalism-Based
    Limits..3**
Section 5. The Tenth Amendment as an External Constraint on the
    Federal Commerce Power...3

**Chapter 5. Federal Limits on State Regulation of Interstate
    Commerce..5**
Section 4. Other Aspects of Federal-State Relationships 5

Chapter 6. Separation of Powers 9
Section 1. Executive Assertions of Power..9
    Executive Power, Immigration, National Security, and Religious
        Bias 9
Section 3. Congressional Authority to Restrain and Enable the
    Executive 18

Chapter 8. Due Process..21
Section 2. Substantive Due Process and Privacy................................21
    Whole Woman's Health et al. v. Hellerstedt, Commissioner, Texas
        Department of State Health Services, et al................................21
Section 4. Textual Guarantees of Economic Liberties: The Takings
    Clause and the Contracts Clause...25

Chapter 9. Equal Protection...27
Section 2. Race Discrimination 27
    Fisher v. University of Texas at Austin et al. 27
Section 3. Sex Discrimination 31
Section 5. The "Fundamental Interests" Branch of Equal Protection.........33

**Chapter 12. Freedom of Speech—Modes of Regulation and
    Standards of Review...37**
Section 1. Content-Based and Content-Neutral Regulations 37
    Speech Versus Conduct in Pricing...37
Section 2. Government's Power to Limit Speech as Quasi-Private Actor....38
    Matal v. Tam 40

**Chapter 13. Beyond Speaking—Compelled Speech, Association,
    Money, and the Media 45**
Section 1. Compelled Speech: The Right *Not* to Speak 45
    National Institute of Family and Life Advocates v. Becerra 45
Section 2. Freedom of Expressive Association 48
Section 3. Money and Political Campaigns 52

Chapter 14. The Religion Clauses: Free Exercise and Establishment 53

Section 3. The Free Exercise of Religion 53

Section 5. Reconciling the Religion Clauses.................................58

    Funding for Religious Entities...58

    Trinity Lutheran Church of Columbia, Inc. v. Comer...........58

TABLE OF CASES

The principal cases are in bold type.

Evenwel v. Abbott, 33
Expressions Hair Design v.
    Schneiderman, 37
**Fisher v. University of Texas at
    Austin et al., 27**
Freytag v. Commissioner, 19
Gill v. Whitford, 34
Heffernan v. City of Paterson, 39
Janus v. American Federation of
    State, County, and Municipal
    Employees, Council 31, 48
Kleindienst v. Mandel, 12
Lucia v. SEC, 18
Masterpiece Cakeshop v. Colorado
    Civil Rights Commission, 53
Matal v. Tam, 40
McDonnell v. United States, 52
Minnesota Voters Alliance v.
    Mansky, 38
Murphy v. National Collegiate
    Athletic Assn., 3
**National Institute of Family and
    Life Advocates v. Becerra, 45**
Sessions v. Morales-Santana, 31
South Dakota v. Wayfair, 5
Spokeo, Inc. v. Robins, 1
Sveen v. Melin, 25
**Trinity Lutheran Church of
    Columbia, Inc. v. Comer, 58**
Trump v. Hawaii, 10
Trump v. International Refugee
    Assistance Project, 9
**Whole Woman's Health et al. v.
    Hellerstedt, Commissioner,
    Texas Department of State
    Health Services, et al., 21**

UNIVERSITY CASEBOOK SERIES®

2018 SUPPLEMENT TO

CONSTITUTIONAL LAW

NINETEENTH EDITION

CHAPTER 1

THE SUPREME COURT'S AUTHORITY AND ROLE

SECTION 4. CONSTITUTIONAL AND PRUDENTIAL LIMITS ON CONSTITUTIONAL ADJUDICATION: THE "CASE OR CONTROVERSY" REQUIREMENTS

Page 55. Add after Note 8, *Congressional power to confer standing*:

In **Spokeo, Inc. v. Robins**, 578 U.S. ___, 136 S.Ct. 1540 (2016), a consumer sued under the Fair Credit Reporting Act, claiming that a website gave out inaccurate credit information about him. The Court held that the consumer could not satisfy the injury-in-fact requirements of Article III by alleging a bare procedural violation of the federal statute. Justice ALITO wrote the opinion: "[The] injury-in-fact requirement requires a plaintiff to allege an injury that is both concrete *and* particularized. [For] an injury to be 'particularized,' it must affect the plaintiff in a personal and individual way. Particularization is necessary to establish injury in fact, but it is not sufficient. [When] we have used the adjective 'concrete,' we have meant to convey the usual meaning of the term—'real,' and not 'abstract.' Webster's Third New International Dictionary 472 (1971); Random House Dictionary of the English Language 305 (1967). Concreteness, therefore, is quite different from particularization. 'Concrete' is not, however, necessarily synonymous with 'tangible.' Although tangible injuries are perhaps easier to recognize, we have confirmed in many of our previous cases that intangible injuries can nevertheless be concrete. [Congress'] role in identifying and elevating intangible harms does not mean that a plaintiff automatically satisfies the injury-in-fact requirement whenever a statute grants a person a statutory right and purports to authorize that person to sue to vindicate that right. Article III standing requires a concrete injury even in the context of a statutory violation. [The] law has long permitted recovery by certain tort victims even if their harms may be difficult to prove or measure. Just as the common law permitted suit in such instances, the violation of a procedural right granted by statute can be sufficient in some circumstances to constitute injury in fact. In other words, a plaintiff in such a case need not allege any *additional* harm beyond the one Congress has identified. In the context of this particular case, these general principles tell us two things: On the one hand, Congress plainly sought to curb the dissemination of false information by adopting procedures designed to decrease that risk. On the other hand, Robins cannot satisfy the demands of Article III by alleging a bare procedural violation. A violation of one of the FCRA's procedural requirements may result in no harm. For example, even if a consumer reporting agency fails to provide the required notice to a user of the agency's consumer information, that information regardless may be entirely accurate. In addition, not all inaccuracies cause harm or present any material risk of harm. An example that comes readily to mind is an incorrect zip code. It is difficult to imagine how the dissemination of an incorrect zip code, without more, could work any concrete harm."

Justice GINSBURG, joined by Justice Sotomayor, dissented, explaining that she would not have remanded: "Judged by what we have said about 'concreteness,' Robins' allegations carry him across the threshold."

CHAPTER 3

THE COMMERCE POWER AND ITS FEDERALISM-BASED LIMITS

SECTION 5. THE TENTH AMENDMENT AS AN EXTERNAL CONSTRAINT ON THE FEDERAL COMMERCE POWER

Page 186. Add after Note 3:

4. ***Anticommandeering as a limit to federal bars on state gambling laws.*** The Professional and Amateur Sports Protection Act (PASPA), enacted in 1992, makes it unlawful for states "to sponsor, operate, advertise, promote, license, or authorize by law or compact . . . a lottery, sweepstakes, or other betting, gambling, or wagering scheme based . . . on" competitive sporting events, 28 U.S.C. § 3702(1). As enacted, PASPA grandfathered in sports gambling in four states, and allowed New Jersey to set up sports gambling in Atlantic City within a year. New Jersey did not take advantage of the option at the time, but in 2012, its legislature authorized sports gambling in Atlantic City and at horseracing tracks. The lower courts held that the law violated PASPA, and the Supreme Court denied certiorari. So in 2014, the New Jersey legislature passed a new law that, instead of affirmatively authorizing sports gambling, repealed state-law provisions that prohibited such schemes. The lower courts again found a PASPA violation.

In **Murphy v. National Collegiate Athletic Assn.**, 585 U.S. ___, 138 S.Ct. 1461 (2018), Justice ALITO wrote the opinion for a 6–3 Court, joined by Chief Justice Roberts and Justices Kennedy, Thomas, Kagan, and Gorsuch. The decision struck down the relevant PASPA provision as unconstitutional commandeering:

"The anticommandeering doctrine may sound arcane, but it is simply the expression of a fundamental structural decision incorporated into the Constitution, *i.e.*, the decision to withhold from Congress the power to issue orders directly to the States. [The] PASPA provision at issue here—prohibiting state authorization of sports gambling—violates the anticommandeering rule. [It] is as if federal officers were installed in state legislative chambers and were armed with the authority to stop legislators from voting on any offending proposals. A more direct affront to state sovereignty is not easy to imagine. Neither respondents nor the United States contends that Congress can compel a State to enact legislation, but they say that prohibiting a State from enacting new laws is another matter. [This] distinction is empty. It was a matter of happenstance that the laws challenged in New York and Printz commanded "affirmative" action as opposed to imposing a prohibition. The basic principle—that Congress cannot issue direct orders to state legislatures—applies in either event. [Respondents] and the United States defend the anti-authorization prohibition on the ground that it constitutes a valid preemption provision, but it is no such thing. Preemption is based on the Supremacy Clause, and that Clause is not an independent grant of legislative power to Congress. [Therefore,] in order for the PASPA provision to preempt state law, it must [represent] the exercise of a power conferred on Congress by the Constitution; pointing to the Supremacy Clause will not do. [And] since the Constitution confers upon Congress the power to regulate individuals, not States, the PASPA provision at issue must be best read as one that regulates private actors.

"[It] is clear that the PASPA provision prohibiting state authorization of sports gambling is not a preemption provision because there is no way in which this provision can be understood as a regulation of private actors. It certainly does not confer any federal rights on private actors interested in conducting sports gambling operations. (It does not give them a federal right to engage in sports gambling.) Nor does it impose any federal restrictions on private actors. [Thus,] there is simply no way to understand the provision prohibiting state authorization as anything other than a direct command to the States."

CHAPTER 5

FEDERAL LIMITS ON STATE REGULATION OF INTERSTATE COMMERCE

SECTION 4. OTHER ASPECTS OF FEDERAL-STATE RELATIONSHIPS

Page 298. Add after discussion of Quill Corp. v. North Dakota:

In **South Dakota v. Wayfair**, 584 U.S. ___, 138 S.Ct. 2080 (2018), the Court overruled Quill's physical presence rule by a 5–4 vote. Justice KENNEDY wrote for the Court, joined by Justices Thomas, Ginsburg, Alito and Gorsuch:

"Quill created an inefficient 'online sales tax loophole' that gives out-of-state businesses an advantage. [Each] year, the physical presence rule becomes further removed from economic reality and results in significant revenue losses to the States. Quill is flawed on its own terms. First, the physical presence rule is not a necessary interpretation of the requirement that a state tax must be applied to an activity with a substantial nexus with the taxing State. Second, Quill creates rather than resolves market distortions. And third, Quill imposes the sort of arbitrary, formalistic distinction that the Court's modern Commerce Clause precedents disavow. [Quill] puts both local businesses and many interstate businesses with physical presence at a competitive disadvantage relative to remote sellers. Remote sellers can avoid the regulatory burdens of tax collection and can offer *de facto* lower prices caused by the widespread failure of consumers to pay the tax on their own. [In] effect, Quill has come to serve as a judicially created tax shelter for businesses that decide to limit their physical presence and still sell their goods and services to a State's consumers—something that has become easier and more prevalent as technology has advanced. Worse still, the rule produces an incentive to avoid physical presence in multiple States. Distortions caused by the desire of businesses to avoid tax collection mean that the market may currently lack storefronts, distribution points, and employment centers that otherwise would be efficient or desirable.

"[Here,] *stare decisis* can no longer support the Court's prohibition of a valid exercise of the States' sovereign power. [While] it can be conceded that Congress has the authority to change the physical presence rule, Congress cannot change the constitutional default rule. It is inconsistent with the Court's proper role to ask Congress to address a false constitutional premise of this Court's own creation. Courts have acted as the front line of review in this limited sphere; and hence it is important that their principles be accurate and logical, whether or not Congress can or will act in response. It is currently the Court, and not Congress, that is limiting the lawful prerogatives of the States. [*Stare decisis*] accommodates only legitimate reliance interests. Here, the tax distortion created by Quill exists in large part because consumers regularly fail to comply with lawful use taxes.

"[In] the absence of Quill, the first prong of the Complete Auto test simply asks whether the tax applies to an activity with a substantial nexus with the taxing State. [Here,] the nexus is clearly sufficient based on both the economic and virtual contacts respondents have with the State. The Act applies only to sellers that deliver more than $100,000 of goods or services into South Dakota or engage in 200 or more separate transactions for the delivery of goods and services into the State on an annual basis. S. B. 106, § 1. This quantity of business could not have occurred unless the seller availed itself of the substantial privilege of carrying on business in South Dakota. And respondents are large, national companies that undoubtedly maintain an extensive virtual presence."

Justice GORSUCH concurred and took the opportunity to cast doubt on the entirety of dormant Commerce Clause jurisprudence: "The Commerce Clause is found in Article I and authorizes *Congress* to regulate interstate commerce. Meanwhile our dormant commerce cases suggest Article III *courts* may invalidate state laws that offend no congressional statute. Whether and how much of this can be squared with the text of the Commerce Clause, justified by *stare decisis*, or defended as misbranded products of federalism or antidiscrimination imperatives flowing from Article IV's Privileges and Immunities Clause are questions for another day."

■ CHIEF JUSTICE ROBERTS dissented, joined by JUSTICES BREYER, SOTOMAYOR, and KAGAN:

"E-commerce has grown into a significant and vibrant part of our national economy against the backdrop of established rules, including the physical-presence rule. Any alteration to those rules with the potential to disrupt the development of such a critical segment of the economy should be undertaken by Congress. The Court should not act on this important question of current economic policy, solely to expiate a mistake it made over 50 years ago. [Nothing] in today's decision precludes Congress from continuing to seek a legislative solution. But by suddenly changing the ground rules, the Court may have waylaid Congress's consideration of the issue. Armed with today's decision, state officials can be expected to redirect their attention from working with Congress on a national solution, to securing new tax revenue from remote retailers.

"[The] Court [breezily] disregards the costs that its decision will impose on retailers. Correctly calculating and remitting sales taxes on all e-commerce sales will likely prove baffling for many retailers. Over 10,000 jurisdictions levy sales taxes, each with 'different tax rates, different rules governing tax-exempt goods and services, different product category definitions, and different standards for determining whether an out-of-state seller has a substantial presence' in the jurisdiction. [The] burden will fall disproportionately on small businesses. One vitalizing effect of the Internet has been connecting small, even 'micro' businesses to potential buyers across the Nation. People starting a business selling their embroidered pillowcases or carved decoys can offer their wares throughout the country—but probably not if they have to figure out the tax due on every sale. And the software said to facilitate compliance is still in its infancy, and its capabilities and expense are subject to debate. The Court's decision today will surely have the effect of dampening opportunities for commerce in a broad range of new markets. A good reason to leave these matters to Congress is that legislators may more directly consider the competing interests at stake. Unlike this Court, Congress has the flexibility to address these questions in a wide variety of ways. [The] Court is of course correct that the Nation's economy has changed dramatically since the time that [Quill] roamed the earth. I fear the Court today is compounding its past error by trying to fix it in a totally different era. I would let Congress decide."

CHAPTER 6

SEPARATION OF POWERS

SECTION 1. EXECUTIVE ASSERTIONS OF POWER

Page 330. Add to end of Section 1:

EXECUTIVE POWER, IMMIGRATION, NATIONAL SECURITY, AND RELIGIOUS BIAS

On January 27, 2017, just after his inauguration, President Donald Trump signed Executive Order No. 13769, "Protecting the Nation from Foreign Terrorist Entry into the United States," 82 Fed. Reg. 8977. The order (EO-1) barred visitors from Iraq, Syria, Iran, Libya, Somalia, Sudan and Yemen from entering the United States for 90 days, suspended entry of Syrian refugees indefinitely, and blocked any other refugees for 120 days. Volunteer lawyers flocked to airports to assist travelers who would be stopped as a result of the order. The American Civil Liberties Union, representing travelers, sued to block the operation of EO-1, alleging among other things that that it was motivated by anti-Muslim bias. The evidence came from statements by Trump as a candidate and by advisors including former New York mayor Rudy Giuliani.

After a federal district in Washington State stayed the operation of EO-1, and the U.S. Court of Appeals for the Ninth Circuit upheld the ruling, Trump, on March 6, 2017, revoked the first order and signed a new, amended Executive Order No. 13780, 82 Fed. Reg. 13209. This second order (EO-2) allowed for case-by-case waivers, exempted travelers who already had visas and green cards, and removed Iraq from the list of covered countries. It stated that the countries had been selected because each "is a state sponsor of terrorism, has been significantly compromised by terrorist organizations, or contains active conflict zones." EO-2 also mandated an executive-branch review of the adequacy of current practices of visa granting. Federal district courts in Hawaii and Maryland issued nationwide preliminary injunctions staying this order, and courts of appeals left those orders in place.

In **Trump v. International Refugee Assistance Project**, 582 U.S. ___, 137 S.Ct. 2080 (2017) (per curiam), the Supreme Court stayed the injunctions and allowed the travel ban to go into effect only with respect to foreign nationals who lacked a "credible claim of a bona fide relationship" with a person or entity in the United States. The court explained that denying entry to a foreign national "who [has] no connection to the United States at all" did "not burden any American party by reason of that party's relationship with the foreign national." It held that "[f]or individuals, a close familial relationship is required. [As] for entities, the relationship must be formal, documented, and formed in the ordinary course, rather than for the purpose of evading EO-2. The students from the designated countries who have been admitted to the University of Hawaii have such a relationship with an American entity. So too would a worker who accepted an offer of employment from an American company or a lecturer invited to address an American audience. Not so someone who enters into a relationship simply to avoid EO-2: For example, a nonprofit group devoted to immigration issues may not contact foreign nationals from the designated countries, add them to client lists, and then secure their entry by claiming injury from their exclusion."

On September 24, 2017, after the temporary order had expired, Trump issued a further Proclamation No. 9645, "Enhancing Vetting Capabilities and Processes for Detecting Attempted Entry Into the United States by Terrorists or Other Public-Safety Threats," 82 Fed. Reg. 45161. The Proclamation placed entry restrictions on certain nationals of Chad, Iran, Iraq, Libya, North Korea, Syria, Yemen, and Venezuela, on the ground that those countries had inadequate systems in place for managing and sharing information about their nationals with the United States. The Proclamation stated that the Department of Homeland Security had made this determination after review in consultation with the State Department and intelligence agencies. The Proclamation suspended entry of all nationals from Iran, North Korea, and Syria, except for Iranians seeking nonimmigrant student and exchange-visitor visas. For Somalia, it suspended entry of nationals seeking immigrant visas and required additional scrutiny of nationals seeking nonimmigrant visas. For Venezuela, the Proclamation limited entry only of certain government officials and their family members on nonimmigrant business or tourist visas. The Proclamation exempted lawful permanent residents and foreign nationals who had been granted asylum, and provided for case-by-case waivers when a foreign national demonstrates undue hardship, and that his entry is in the national interest and would not pose a threat to public safety. The Proclamation further directed DHS to assess on a continuing basis whether entry restrictions should be modified or continued.

The State of Hawaii, three individuals (Dr. Ismail Elshikh, John Doe #1, and John Doe #2), and the Muslim Association of Hawaii challenged the proclamation, and the district court granted a nationwide preliminary injunction barring its enforcement. The Ninth Circuit upheld the district court on statutory grounds, and did not reach the plaintiffs' Establishment Clause claim.

In **Trump v. Hawaii**, 585 U.S. ___, 138 S.Ct. 2392 (2018), the Court reversed in an opinion by Chief Justice ROBERTS. First it addressed the statutory issues, holding that the president's actions were authorized by 8 U.S.C. §§ 1182(f), which "grants the President broad discretion to suspend the entry of aliens into the United States." The court held that "the President lawfully exercised that discretion based on his findings—following a worldwide, multi-agency review—that entry of the covered aliens would be detrimental to the national interest."

Turning to the constitutional issues, the Court first held that the plaintiffs had standing because "a person's interest in being united with his relatives is sufficiently concrete and particularized to form the basis of an Article III injury in fact." The Court then rejected the plaintiffs'

Establishment Clause claim that the Proclamation "singl[ed] out Muslims for disfavored treatment" and "operate[d] as a 'religious gerrymander,' in part because most of the countries covered by the Proclamation have Muslim-majority populations."

Chief Justice Roberts continued: "At the heart of plaintiffs' case is a series of statements by the President and his advisers casting doubt on the official objective of the Proclamation. For example, while a candidate on the campaign trail, the President published a 'Statement on Preventing Muslim Immigration' that called for a 'total and complete shutdown of Muslims entering the United States until our country's representatives can figure out what is going on.'" That statement remained on his campaign website until May 2017. Then-candidate Trump also stated that 'Islam hates us' and asserted that the United States was 'having problems with Muslims coming into the country.' Shortly after being elected, when asked whether violence in Europe had affected his plans to 'ban Muslim immigration,' the President replied, 'You know my plans. All along, I've been proven to be right.' One week after his inauguration, the President issued EO-1. In a television interview, one of the President's campaign advisers [editors' note: Rudy Giuliani] explained that when the President 'first announced it, he said, "Muslim ban." He called me up. He said, "Put a commission together. Show me the right way to do it legally."' The adviser said he assembled a group of Members of Congress and lawyers that 'focused on, instead of religion, danger. . . . [The order] is based on places where there [is] substantial evidence that people are sending terrorists into our country.'

"Plaintiffs also note that after issuing EO-2 to replace EO-1, the President expressed regret that his prior order had been 'watered down' and called for a 'much tougher version of his 'Travel Ban.' Shortly before the release of the Proclamation, he stated that the 'travel ban . . . should be far larger, tougher, and more specific,' but 'stupidly that would not be politically correct.' More recently, on November 29, 2017, the President retweeted links to three anti-Muslim propaganda videos. In response to questions about those videos, the President's deputy press secretary denied that the President thinks Muslims are a threat to the United States, explaining that 'the President has been talking about these security issues for years now, from the campaign trail to the White House' and 'has addressed these issues with the travel order that he issued earlier this year and the companion proclamation.'

"[The] issue before us is not whether to denounce the statements. It is instead the significance of those statements in reviewing a Presidential directive, neutral on its face, addressing a matter within the core of executive responsibility. In doing so, we must consider not only the statements of a particular President, but also the authority of the Presidency itself.

"The case before us differs in numerous respects from the conventional Establishment Clause claim. Unlike the typical suit involving religious displays or school prayer, plaintiffs seek to invalidate a national security directive regulating the entry of aliens abroad. Their claim accordingly raises a number of delicate issues regarding the scope of the constitutional right and the manner of proof. The Proclamation, moreover, is facially neutral toward religion. Plaintiffs therefore ask the Court to probe the sincerity of the stated justifications for the policy by reference to extrinsic statements— many of which were made before the President took the oath of office. These various aspects of plaintiffs' challenge inform our standard of review.

"For more than a century, this Court has recognized that the admission and exclusion of foreign nationals is a fundamental sovereign attribute exercised by the Government's political departments largely immune from judicial control. Because decisions in these matters may implicate relations with foreign powers, or involve classifications defined in the light of changing political and economic circumstances, such judgments are frequently of a character more appropriate to either the Legislature or the Executive. Nonetheless, although foreign nationals seeking admission have no constitutional right to entry, this Court has engaged in a circumscribed judicial inquiry when the denial of a visa allegedly burdens the constitutional rights of a U.S. citizen.

"In Kleindienst v. Mandel, 408 U.S. 753 (1972), the Attorney General denied admission to a Belgian journalist and self-described 'revolutionary Marxist,' Ernest Mandel, who had been invited to speak at a conference at Stanford University. [We] held that 'when the Executive exercises this [delegated] power negatively on the basis of a facially legitimate and bona fide reason, the courts will neither look behind the exercise of that discretion, nor test it by balancing its justification' against the asserted constitutional interests of U.S. citizens. [Mandel's] narrow standard of review has particular force in admission and immigration cases that overlap with the area of national security.

"[A] conventional application of Mandel, asking only whether the policy is facially legitimate and bona fide, would put an end to our review. [For] our purposes today, we assume that we may look behind the face of the Proclamation to the extent of applying rational basis review. That standard of review considers whether the entry policy is plausibly related to the Government's stated objective to protect the country and improve vetting processes. As a result, we may consider plaintiffs' extrinsic evidence, but will uphold the policy so long as it can reasonably be understood to result from a justification independent of unconstitutional grounds.[1]

"[The] Court hardly ever strikes down a policy as illegitimate under rational basis scrutiny. On the few occasions where we have done so, a common thread has been that the laws at issue lack any purpose other than a bare [desire] to harm a politically unpopular group. In one case, we invalidated a local zoning ordinance that required a special permit for group homes for the intellectually disabled, but not for other facilities such as fraternity houses or hospitals. Cleburne v. Cleburne [p. 799]. And in another case, this Court overturned a state constitutional amendment that denied gays and lesbians access to the protection of antidiscrimination laws. The

---

[1]   The dissent finds 'perplexing' the application of rational basis review in this context. But what is far more problematic is the dissent's assumption that courts should review immigration policies, diplomatic sanctions, and military actions under the *de novo* 'reasonable observer' inquiry applicable to cases involving holiday displays and graduation ceremonies.

[amendment] seemed 'inexplicable by anything but animus.' Romer v. Evans [p. 553].

"The Proclamation does not fit this pattern. It cannot be said that it is impossible to discern a relationship to legitimate state interests or that the policy is 'inexplicable by anything but animus. [Because] there is persuasive evidence that the entry suspension has a legitimate grounding in national security concerns, quite apart from any religious hostility, we must accept that independent justification.

"The Proclamation is expressly premised on legitimate purposes: preventing entry of nationals who cannot be adequately vetted and inducing other nations to improve their practices. The text says nothing about religion. [Five] of the seven nations currently included in the Proclamation have Muslim-majority populations. Yet that fact alone does not support an inference of religious hostility, given that the policy covers just 8% of the world's Muslim population and is limited to countries that were previously designated by Congress or prior administrations as posing national security risks. The Proclamation, moreover, reflects the results of a worldwide review process undertaken by multiple Cabinet officials and their agencies. Plaintiffs seek to discredit the findings of the review, pointing to deviations from the review's baseline criteria resulting in the inclusion of Somalia and omission of Iraq. But as the Proclamation explains, in each case the determinations were justified by the distinct conditions in each country.

"[More] fundamentally, plaintiffs and the dissent [suggest] that the policy is overbroad and does little to serve national security interests. But we cannot substitute our own assessment for the Executive's predictive judgments on such matters. [While] we of course 'do not defer to the Government's reading of the First Amendment,' the Executive's evaluation of the underlying facts is entitled to appropriate weight, particularly in the context of litigation involving 'sensitive and weighty interests of national security and foreign affairs.' Humanitarian Law Project [p. 1199].

"Finally, the dissent invokes Korematsu. Whatever rhetorical advantage the dissent may see in doing so, Korematsu has nothing to do with this case. The forcible relocation of U.S. citizens to concentration camps, solely and explicitly on the basis of race, is objectively unlawful and outside the scope of Presidential authority. But it is wholly inapt to liken that morally repugnant order to a facially neutral policy denying certain foreign nationals the privilege of admission. The entry suspension is an act that is well within executive authority and could have been taken by any other President—the only question is evaluating the actions of this particular President in promulgating an otherwise valid Proclamation.

"The dissent's reference to Korematsu, however, affords this Court the opportunity to make express what is already obvious: Korematsu was gravely wrong the day it was decided, has been overruled in the court of history, and—to be clear—'has no place in law under the Constitution.' Id. (Jackson, J., dissenting).

Justice KENNEDY joined the opinion fully and concurred briefly in what would be his last opinion before announcing his retirement the following day: "There may be some common ground between the opinions in this case, in that the Court does acknowledge that in some instances, governmental action may be subject to judicial review to determine whether or not it is 'inexplicable by anything but animus,' Romer, which in this case would be animosity to a religion. Whether judicial proceedings may properly continue in this case, in light of the substantial deference that is and must be accorded to the Executive in the conduct of foreign affairs, and in light of today's decision, is a matter to be addressed in the first instance on remand. And even if further proceedings are permitted, it would be necessary to determine that any discovery and other preliminary matters would not themselves intrude on the foreign affairs power of the Executive.

"[There] are numerous instances in which the statements and actions of Government officials are not subject to judicial scrutiny or intervention. That does not mean those officials are free to disregard the Constitution and the rights it proclaims and protects. [The very fact that an official may have broad discretion, discretion free from judicial scrutiny, makes it all the more imperative for him or her to adhere to the Constitution and to its meaning and its promise. [It] is an urgent necessity that officials adhere to [the First Amendment] in all their actions, even in the sphere of foreign affairs. An anxious world must know that our Government remains committed always to the liberties the Constitution seeks to preserve and protect, so that freedom extends outward, and lasts."

Justice BREYER, joined by Justice Kagan, dissented: "If [the Proclamation's] promulgation or content was significantly affected by religious animus against Muslims, it would violate the relevant statute or the First Amendment itself. If, however, its sole *ratio decidendi* was one of national security, then it would be unlikely to violate either the statute or the Constitution. [Members] of the Court principally disagree about the answer to this question, *i.e.,* about whether or the extent to which religious animus played a significant role in the Proclamation's promulgation or content. [The] Proclamation's elaborate system of exemptions and waivers can and should help us answer this question. [If] the Government is applying the exemption and waiver provisions as written, then its argument for the Proclamation's lawfulness is strengthened. [Since] the case-by-case exemptions and waivers apply without regard to the individual's religion, application of that system would help make clear that the Proclamation does not deny visas to numerous Muslim individuals (from those countries) who do not pose a security threat. [If] the Government is *not* applying the system of exemptions and waivers that the Proclamation contains, then its argument for the Proclamation's lawfulness becomes significantly weaker. [If] the Government is not applying the Proclamation's exemption and waiver system, the claim that the Proclamation is a 'Muslim ban,' rather than a 'security-based' ban, becomes much stronger. [Unfortunately] there is evidence that supports the second possibility, *i.e.,* that the Government is not applying the Proclamation as written. The Proclamation provides that the Secretary of State and the Secretary of Homeland Security 'shall coordinate to adopt guidance' for consular officers to follow when deciding whether to grant a waiver. Yet, to my knowledge, no guidance has issued.

[The] State Department reported that during the Proclamation's first month, two waivers were approved out of 6,555 eligible applicants. [The] Government claims that number increased from 2 to 430 during the first four months of implementation. That number, 430, however, when compared with the number of pre-Proclamation visitors, accounts for a miniscule percentage of those likely eligible for visas, in such categories as persons requiring medical treatment, academic visitors, students, family members, and others belonging to groups that, when considered as a group (rather than case by case), would not seem to pose security threats. [The] Government has not had an opportunity to respond, and a court has not had an opportunity to decide. But, given the importance of the decision in this case, the need for assurance that the Proclamation does not rest upon a 'Muslim ban,' and the assistance in deciding the issue that answers to the exemption and waiver questions may provide, I would send this case back to the District Court for further proceedings. And, I would leave the injunction in effect while the matter is litigated. Regardless, the Court's decision today leaves the District Court free to explore these issues on remand. If this Court must decide the question without this further litigation, I would, on balance, find the evidence of antireligious bias, including statements on a website taken down only after the President issued the two executive orders preceding the Proclamation, along with the other statements also set forth in Justice Sotomayor's opinion, a sufficient basis to set the Proclamation aside."

Justice SOTOMAYOR dissented, joined by Justice Ginsburg: "The United States of America is a Nation built upon the promise of religious liberty. [The] Court's decision today fails to safeguard that fundamental principle. It leaves undisturbed a policy first advertised openly and unequivocally as a 'total and complete shutdown of Muslims entering the United States' because the policy now masquerades behind a façade of national-security concerns. But this repackaging does little to cleanse [the] Proclamation of the appearance of discrimination that the President's words have created. [To] determine whether plaintiffs have proved an Establishment Clause violation, the Court asks whether a reasonable observer would view the government action as enacted for the purpose of disfavoring a religion. In answering that question, this Court has generally considered the text of the government policy, its operation, and any available evidence regarding the historical background of the decision under challenge, the specific series of events leading to the enactment or official policy in question, and the legislative or administrative history, including contemporaneous statements made by the decisionmaker. Lukumi. At the same time, however, courts must take care not to engage in "any judicial psychoanalysis of a drafter's heart of hearts. Although the majority briefly recounts a few of the statements and background events that form the basis of plaintiffs' constitutional challenge, that highly abridged account does not tell even half of the story. The full record paints a far more harrowing picture, from which a reasonable observer would readily conclude that the Proclamation was motivated by hostility and animus toward the Muslim faith.

"During his Presidential campaign, then-candidate Donald Trump pledged that, if elected, he would ban Muslims from entering the United States. [On] December 8, 2015, Trump justified his proposal during a television interview by noting that President Franklin D. Roosevelt 'did the same thing' with respect to the internment of Japanese Americans during World War II. In January 2016, during a Republican primary debate, Trump was asked whether he wanted to 'rethink [his] position' on 'banning Muslims from entering the country.' He answered, 'No.' A month later, at a rally in South Carolina, Trump told an apocryphal story about United States General John J. Pershing killing a large group of Muslim insurgents in the Philippines with bullets dipped in pigs' blood in the early 1900's. In March 2016, he expressed his belief that 'Islam hates us. . . . [W]e can't allow people coming into this country who have this hatred of the United States . . . [a]nd of people that are not Muslim.' That same month, Trump asserted that '[w]e're having problems with the Muslims, and we're having problems with Muslims coming into the country.' He therefore called for surveillance of mosques in the United States, blaming terrorist attacks on Muslims' lack of 'assimilation' and their commitment to 'sharia law.'

"[As] Trump's presidential campaign progressed, he began to describe his policy proposal in slightly different terms. In June 2016, for instance, he characterized the policy proposal as a suspension of immigration from countries 'where there's a proven history of terrorism.' [A] month before the 2016 election, Trump reiterated that his proposed 'Muslim ban' had 'morphed into a[n] extreme vetting from certain areas of the world.'

"On January 27, 2017, one week after taking office, President Trump signed [EO-1] As he signed it, President Trump read the title, looked up, and said "We all know what that means." That same day, President Trump explained to the media that, under EO-1, Christians would be given priority for entry as refugees into the United States. In particular, he bemoaned the fact that in the past, '[i]f you were a Muslim [refugee from Syria] you could come in, but if you were a Christian, it was almost impossible.' Considering that past policy "very unfair," President Trump explained that EO-1 was designed 'to help' the Christians in Syria. [After] EO-2 was issued, the White House Press Secretary told reporters that, by issuing EO-2, President Trump 'continue[d] to deliver on . . . his most significant campaign promises.' [While] litigation over EO-2 was ongoing, President Trump repeatedly made statements alluding to a desire to keep Muslims out of the country. [In] June 2017, the President [tweeted]: 'People, the lawyers and the courts can call it whatever they want, but I am calling it what we need and what it is, a TRAVEL BAN!' *Id.*, at 132–133. He added: 'That's right, we need a TRAVEL BAN for certain DANGEROUS countries, not some politically correct term that won't help us protect our people!' [On] November 29, 2017, President Trump retweeted three anti-Muslim videos. [Those] videos were initially tweeted by a British political party whose mission is to oppose 'all alien and destructive politic[al] or religious doctrines, including . . . Islam.' When asked about these videos, the White House Deputy Press Secretary connected them to the Proclamation, responding that the 'President has been talking about these security issues for years now, from the campaign trail to the White House' and 'has addressed these issues with the travel order that he issued earlier this year and the companion proclamation.'

"[Taking] all the relevant evidence together, a reasonable observer would conclude that the Proclamation was driven primarily by anti-Muslim animus, rather than by the Government's asserted national-security justifications. [Moreover,] despite several opportunities to do so, President Trump has never disavowed any of his prior statements about Islam. [Ultimately,] new window dressing cannot conceal an unassailable fact: the words of the President and his advisers create the strong perception that the Proclamation is contaminated by impermissible discriminatory animus against Islam and its followers.

"[The] majority rightly declines to apply Mandel's narrow standard of review. [In] doing so, however, the Court, without explanation or precedential support, limits its review of the Proclamation to rational-basis scrutiny. That approach is perplexing, given that in other Establishment Clause cases, including those involving claims of religious animus or discrimination, this Court has applied a more stringent standard of review. [But] even under rational-basis review, the Proclamation must fall [because it] is divorced from any factual context from which we could discern a relationship to legitimate state interests, and its sheer breadth is so discontinuous with the reasons offered for it that the policy is inexplicable by anything but animus. Romer. [It] is of no moment that the Proclamation also includes minor restrictions on two non-Muslim majority countries, North Korea and Venezuela, or that the Government has removed a few Muslim-majority countries from the list of covered countries since EO-1 was issued. [The] inclusion of North Korea and Venezuela, and the removal of other countries, simply reflect subtle efforts to start 'talking territory instead of Muslim,' precisely so the Executive Branch could evade criticism or legal consequences for the Proclamation's otherwise clear targeting of Muslims. The Proclamation's effect on North Korea and Venezuela, for example, is insubstantial, if not entirely symbolic. [The] worldwide review does little to break the clear connection between the Proclamation and the President's anti-Muslim statements. [The] majority empowers the President to hide behind an administrative review process that the Government refuses to disclose to the public. [Evidence] of which we can take judicial notice indicates that the multiagency review process could not have been very thorough. [The] September 2017 report the Government produced after its review process was a mere 17 pages. [That] the Government's analysis of the vetting practices of hundreds of countries boiled down to such a short document raises serious questions about the legitimacy of the President's proclaimed national-security rationale. [Congress also] has already erected a statutory scheme that fulfills the putative national-security interests the Government now puts forth to justify the Proclamation. [Several] former national-security officials from both political parties [have] advised that the Proclamation and its predecessor orders 'do not advance the national-security or foreign policy interests of the United States, and in fact do serious harm to those interests.' Brief for Former National Security Officials as *Amici Curiae*.

"[Just] weeks ago, the Court rendered its decision in Masterpiece Cakeshop [Supplement p. 53], which applied the bedrock principles of religious neutrality and tolerance in considering a First Amendment challenge to government action. [In] both instances, the question is whether a government actor exhibited tolerance and neutrality in reaching a decision that affects individuals' fundamental religious freedom. But unlike in Masterpiece, where a state civil rights commission was found to have acted without the neutrality that the Free Exercise Clause requires, the government actors in this case will not be held accountable for breaching the First Amendment's guarantee of religious neutrality and tolerance. Unlike in Masterpiece, where the majority considered the state commissioners' statements about religion to be persuasive evidence of unconstitutional government action, the majority here completely sets aside the President's charged statements about Muslims as irrelevant. That holding erodes the foundational principles of religious tolerance that the Court elsewhere has so emphatically protected, and it tells members of minority religions in our country 'that they are outsiders, not full members of the political community.'

"Today's holding is all the more troubling given the stark parallels between the reasoning of this case and that of *Korematsu.* [As] here, the Government invoked an ill-defined national-security threat to justify an exclusionary policy of sweeping proportion. As here, the exclusion order was rooted in dangerous stereotypes about, *inter alia*, a particular group's supposed inability to assimilate and desire to harm the United States. As here, the Government was unwilling to reveal its own intelligence agencies' views of the alleged security concerns to the very citizens it purported to protect. And as here, there was strong evidence that impermissible hostility and animus motivated the Government's policy.

"[Today,] the Court takes the important step of finally overruling Korematsu. [This] formal repudiation of a shameful precedent is laudable and long overdue. But it does not make the majority's decision here acceptable or right. By blindly accepting the Government's misguided invitation to sanction a discriminatory policy motivated by animosity toward a disfavored group, all in the name of a superficial claim of national security, the Court redeploys the same dangerous logic underlying Korematsu and merely replaces one gravely wrong decision with another."

SECTION 3. CONGRESSIONAL AUTHORITY TO RESTRAIN AND ENABLE THE EXECUTIVE

Page 395. Add to the end of Note 1, *Appointment of executive officers*:

Lucia v. SEC, 585 U.S. ___, 138 S.Ct. 2044 (2018), involved a challenge to the constitutionality of SEC's appointment of its administrative law judges by staff decision rather than by the commissioners. The issue was whether the ALJs are "officers of the United States" who must by appointed by the President, a court of law, or a head of department under the Appointments Clause, Art. II, § 2, cl. 2, or merely employees, not subject to that Clause's requirement. Justice KAGAN, writing for the Court in a decision joined by Chief Justice Roberts and Justices Kennedy, Thomas, Alito and Gorsuch, held that the ALJs were officers under the clause and thus unconstitutionally appointed because not appointed by heads of department, which would include the commissioners but not their staff.

The decision relied upon the reasoning in a prior decision, Freytag v. Commissioner, 501 U.S. 868 (1991), which had held that special trial judges appointed by the Tax Court were officers subject to the Clause, but were constitutionally appointed because the Tax Court, although an Article I court and not an Article III court, is a court of law for Appointments Clause purposes: "[In] Freytag we applied the unadorned 'significant authority' test to adjudicative officials who are near-carbon copies of the Commission's ALJs [and] held that the Tax Court's special trial judges (STJs) are officers, not mere employees. [The] Court said: STJs 'take testimony, conduct trials, rule on the admissibility of evidence, and have the power to enforce compliance with discovery orders.' And the Court observed that STJs 'exercise significant discretion.' That fact meant they were officers, even when their decisions were not final." Justice Kagan observed that SEC ALJs have the same features, and "at the close of those proceedings, [issue] decisions much like that in Freytag—except with potentially more independent effect."

Justice THOMAS concurred, joined by Justice Gorsuch, to say that, "while precedents like Freytag discuss what is *sufficient* to make someone an officer of the United States, our precedents have never clearly defined what is *necessary*. I would resolve that question based on the original public meaning of 'Officers of the United States.' To the Founders, this term encompassed all federal civil officials with responsibility for an ongoing statutory duty [no] matter how important or significant the duty." Justice BREYER, joined by Justices Ginsburg and Sotomayor, concurred on statutory grounds only and dissented on the remedy: "I cannot answer the constitutional question that the majority answers without knowing the answer to a different, embedded constitutional question: [the] constitutionality of the statutory for cause removal protections that Congress provided for administrative law judges."

Justice SOTOMAYOR, joined by Justice Ginsburg, dissented: "To provide guidance to Congress and the Executive Branch, I would hold that one requisite component of 'significant authority' is the ability to make final, binding decisions on behalf of the Government. Accordingly, a person who merely advises and provides recommendations to an officer would not herself qualify as an officer." Under that standard, she would have held "that Commission ALJs are not officers because they lack final decisionmaking authority," as their decisions are always subject to the Commission's de novo review.

On July 10, 2018, just a few weeks after Lucia was decided, President Donald Trump issued an executive order placing all ALJs in the executive branch into the category of "excepted" civil service employees, meaning that ALJs would no longer be appointed on the basis of performance in competitive civil service examinations. The order explained the departure from historical practice with direct reference to Lucia: "Lucia may also raise questions about the method of appointing ALJs, including whether competitive examination and competitive service selection procedures are compatible with the discretion an agency head must possess under the Appointments Clause in selecting ALJs. Regardless of whether those procedures would violate the Appointments Clause as applied to certain ALJs, there are sound policy reasons to take steps to eliminate doubt regarding the constitutionality of the method of appointing officials who discharge such significant duties and exercise such significant discretion." Does Lucia in fact support President Trump's order, even with the caveats the order includes?

CHAPTER 8

DUE PROCESS

SECTION 2. SUBSTANTIVE DUE PROCESS AND PRIVACY

Page 544. Add after Gonzales v. Carhart:

Whole Woman's Health et al. v. Hellerstedt, Commissioner, Texas Department of State Health Services, et al.

___ U.S. ___, 136 S.Ct. 2292, 195 L.Ed.2d 665 (2016).

■ JUSTICE BREYER delivered the opinion of the Court, in which JUSTICES KENNEDY, GINSBURG, KAGAN, and SOTOMAYOR joined.

We must here decide whether two provisions of Texas' House Bill 2 violate the Federal Constitution as interpreted in Casey. The first provision, which we shall call the *"admitting-privileges requirement,"* says that "[a] physician performing or inducing an abortion must, on the date the abortion is performed or induced, have active admitting privileges at a hospital that is located not further than 30 miles from the location at which the abortion is performed or induced." [T]he second provision, which we shall call the *"surgical-center requirement,"* says that "the minimum standards for an abortion facility must be equivalent to the minimum standards adopted under [the Texas Health and Safety Code section] for ambulatory surgical centers."

We conclude that neither of these provisions confers medical benefits sufficient to justify the burdens upon access that each imposes.

The rule announced in Casey [requires] that courts consider the burdens a law imposes on abortion access together with the benefits.

[The] Court, when determining the constitutionality of laws regulating abortion procedures, has placed considerable weight upon evidence and argument presented in judicial proceedings. In Casey, for example, we relied heavily on the District Court's factual findings and the research-based submissions of *amici*. [And] Gonzales [said] that the *"Court retains an independent constitutional duty to review factual findings where constitutional rights are at stake." Ibid.* (emphasis added).

[The] relevant statute here does not set forth any legislative findings. Rather, one is left to infer that the legislature sought to further a constitutionally acceptable objective (namely, protecting women's health). For a district court to give significant weight to evidence in the judicial record in these circumstances is consistent with this Court's case law.

[The] purpose of the admitting-privileges requirement is to help ensure that women have easy access to a hospital should complications arise during an abortion procedure. But the District Court found that it brought about no such health-related benefit.

[The] evidence upon which the court based this conclusion included, among other things:

- A collection of at least five peer-reviewed studies on abortion complications in the first trimester, showing that the highest rate of major complications—including those complications requiring hospital admission—was less than one-quarter of 1%.

- Figures in three peer-reviewed studies showing that the highest complication rate found for the much rarer second trimester abortion was less than one-half of 1% (0.45% or about 1 out of about 200).

- Expert testimony to the effect that complications rarely require hospital admission, much less immediate transfer to a hospital from an outpatient clinic.

- Expert testimony stating that "it is extremely unlikely that a patient will experience a serious complication at the clinic that requires emergent hospitalization" and "in the rare case in which [one does], the quality of care that the patient receives is not affected by whether the abortion provider has admitting privileges at the hospital."

- Expert testimony stating that in respect to surgical abortion patients who do suffer complications requiring hospitalization, most of these complications occur in the days after the abortion, not on the spot.

- Expert testimony stating that a delay before the onset of complications is also expected for medical abortions, as "abortifacient drugs take time to exert their effects, and thus the abortion itself almost always occurs after the patient has left the abortion facility."

- Some experts added that, if a patient needs a hospital in the day or week following her abortion, she will likely seek medical attention at the hospital nearest her home.

We have found nothing in Texas' record evidence that shows that, compared to prior law (which required a "working arrangement" with a doctor with admitting privileges), the new law advanced Texas' legitimate interest in protecting women's health.

[When] directly asked at oral argument whether Texas knew of a single instance in which the new requirement would have helped even one woman obtain better treatment, Texas admitted that there was no evidence in the record of such a case.

At the same time, the record evidence indicates that the admitting-privileges requirement places a "substantial obstacle in the path of a woman's choice." Casey. [As] of the time the admitting-privileges requirement began to be enforced, the number of facilities providing abortions dropped in half from about 40 to about 20. Eight abortion clinics closed in the months leading up to the requirement's effective date.

Eleven more closed on the day the admitting-privileges requirement took effect.

[In] our view, the record contains sufficient evidence that the admitting-privileges requirement led to the closure of half of Texas' clinics, or thereabouts. Those closures meant fewer doctors, longer waiting times, and increased crowding.

[There] is considerable evidence in the record supporting the District Court's findings indicating that the statutory provision requiring all abortion facilities to meet all surgical-center standards does not benefit patients and is not necessary.

[The] record makes clear that the surgical-center requirement provides no benefit when complications arise in the context of an abortion produced through medication. That is because, in such a case, complications would almost always arise only after the patient has left the facility. The record also contains evidence indicating that abortions taking place in an abortion facility are safe—indeed, safer than numerous procedures that take place outside hospitals and to which Texas does not apply its surgical-center requirements.

[Nationwide], childbirth is 14 times more likely than abortion to result in death, but Texas law allows a midwife to oversee childbirth in the patient's own home. Colonoscopy, a procedure that typically takes place outside a hospital (or surgical center) setting, has a mortality rate 10 times higher than an abortion. (The mortality rate for liposuction, another outpatient procedure, is 28 times higher than the mortality rate for abortion.) Medical treatment after an incomplete miscarriage often involves a procedure identical to that involved in a nonmedical abortion, but it often takes place outside a hospital or surgical center. And Texas partly or wholly grandfathers (or waives in whole or in part the surgical-center requirement for) about two-thirds of the facilities to which the surgical-center standards apply. But it neither grandfathers nor provides waivers for any of the facilities that perform abortions.

Moreover, many surgical-center requirements are inappropriate as applied to surgical abortions.

[The] record provides adequate evidentiary support for the District Court's conclusion that the surgical-center requirement places a substantial obstacle in the path of women seeking an abortion. The parties stipulated that the requirement would further reduce the number of abortion facilities available to seven or eight facilities, located in Houston, Austin, San Antonio, and Dallas/Fort Worth.

[Common] sense suggests that, more often than not, a physical facility that satisfies a certain physical demand will not be able to meet five times that demand without expanding or otherwise incurring significant costs.

[More] fundamentally, in the face of no threat to women's health, Texas seeks to force women to travel long distances to get abortions in crammedto-capacity super-facilities. Patients seeking these services are less likely to get the kind of individualized attention, serious conversation, and emotional support that doctors at less taxed facilities may have offered.

■ JUSTICE GINSBURG, concurring.

The Texas law called H. B. 2 inevitably will reduce the number of clinics and doctors allowed to provide abortion services.

[Given] those realities, it is beyond rational belief that H. B. 2 could genuinely protect the health of women, and certain that the law would simply make it more difficult for them to obtain abortions." When a State severely limits access to safe and legal procedures, women in desperate circumstances may resort to unlicensed rogue practitioners, *faute de mieux*, at great risk to their health and safety. Targeted Regulation of Abortion Providers laws like H. B. 2 that do little or nothing for health, but rather strew impediments to abortion, cannot survive judicial inspection.

■ JUSTICE THOMAS, dissenting.

[Whatever] scrutiny the majority applies to Texas' law, it bears little resemblance to the undue-burden test the Court articulated in Casey.

First, today's decision requires courts to "consider the burdens a law imposes on abortion access together with the benefits those laws confer." Second, today's opinion tells the courts that, when the law's justifications are medically uncertain, they need not defer to the legislature, and must instead assess medical justifications for abortion restrictions by scrutinizing the record themselves. Finally, even if a law imposes no "substantial obstacle" to women's access to abortions, the law now must have more than a "reasonabl[e] relat[ion] to a legitimate state interest." These precepts are nowhere to be found in Casey or its successors, and transform the undue-burden test to something much more akin to strict scrutiny.

■ JUSTICE ALITO, with whom THE CHIEF JUSTICE and JUSTICE THOMAS join, dissenting.

[While] there can be no doubt that H. B. 2 caused some clinics to cease operation, the absence of proof regarding the reasons for particular closures is a problem because some clinics have or may have closed for [reasons] other than the two H. B. 2 requirements at issue here.

[Even] if the District Court had properly filtered out immaterial closures, its analysis would have been incomplete for a second reason. Petitioners offered scant evidence on the capacity of the clinics that are able to comply with the admitting privileges and ASC requirements, or on those clinics' geographic distribution. Reviewing the evidence in the record, it is far from clear that there has been a material impact on access to abortion.

[The] other potential obstacle to abortion access is the distribution of facilities throughout the State. [If] the only clinics in the State were those that would have remained open if the judgment of the Fifth Circuit had not been enjoined, roughly 95% of the women of reproductive age in the State would live within 150 miles of an open facility (or lived outside that range before H. B. 2).

[We] should decline to hold that these statistics justify the facial invalidation of the H. B. 2 requirements.

SECTION 4. TEXTUAL GUARANTEES OF ECONOMIC LIBERTIES: THE TAKINGS CLAUSE AND THE CONTRACTS CLAUSE

Page 641. Add after Note 4:

5. ***The Contracts Clause and originalism.*** In 2002, Minnesota enacted a law specifying that on divorce, a spouse designated as the revocable beneficiary of a life insurance policy or similar asset would cease to be the beneficiary unless the other spouse specifically re-named him or her. A spouse who was married in 1997 and divorced in 2007, and who would not have collected under the statute after her spouse's 2011 death, claimed that she should collect the life insurance because the state law impaired the life-insurance contract. Citing Spannaus, the Court in **Sveen v. Melin**, ___ U.S. ___, 138 S.Ct. 1815 (2018), rejected the claim and upheld the law. Justice KAGAN wrote for an 8–1 Court: "Minnesota's revocation-on-divorce statute does not substantially impair pre-existing contractual arrangements. True enough that in revoking a beneficiary designation, the law makes a significant change. As Melin says, the whole point of buying life insurance is to provide the proceeds to the named beneficiary. But three aspects of Minnesota's law, taken together, defeat Melin's argument that the change it effected severely impaired her ex-husband's contract. First, the statute is designed to reflect a policyholder's intent—and so to support, rather than impair, the contractual scheme. Second, the law is unlikely to disturb any policyholder's expectations because it does no more than a divorce court could always have done. And third, the statute supplies a mere default rule, which the policyholder can undo in a moment. Indeed, Minnesota's revocation statute stacks up well against laws that this Court upheld against Contracts Clause challenges as far back as the early 1800s."

Justice GORSUCH dissented: "Because legislation often disrupts existing social arrangements, it usually applies only prospectively. [When] it comes to legislation affecting contracts, the Constitution hardens the presumption of prospectivity into a mandate. [In] the Contracts Clause the framers were absolute. [When] some delegates at the Constitutional Convention sought softer language, James Madison acknowledged the 'inconvenience' a categorical rule could sometimes entail 'but thought on the whole it would be overbalanced by the utility of it.' Kmiec & McGinnis, The Contract Clause: A Return to the Original Understanding, 14 Hastings Const. L. Q. 525, 529–530 (1987). For much of its history, this Court construed the Contracts Clause in this light. [More] recently, though, the Court has charted a different course. Our modern cases permit a state to substantially impair a contractual obligation in pursuit of a significant and legitimate public purpose so long as the impairment is reasonable. That test seems hard to square with the Constitution's original public meaning. After all, the Constitution does not speak of 'substantial' impairments—it bars 'any' impairment. Under a balancing approach, too, how are the people to know today whether their lawful contracts will be enforced tomorrow, or instead undone by a legislative majority with different sympathies? Should we worry that a balancing test risks investing judges with discretion to choose which contracts to enforce—a discretion that might be exercised with an eye to the identity (and popularity) of the parties or contracts at hand? How are judges supposed to balance the often radically incommensurate goods found in contracts and legislation? [Many] critics have raised serious objections along these and other lines. They deserve a thoughtful reply, if not in this case then in another."

CHAPTER 9

EQUAL PROTECTION

SECTION 2. RACE DISCRIMINATION

Page 733. Add to end of Note 8:

Fisher v. University of Texas at Austin et al.
576 U.S. ___, 136 S.Ct. 2198, 195 L.Ed.2d 511 (2016).

■ JUSTICE KENNEDY delivered the opinion of the Court.

The Court is asked once again to consider whether the race-conscious admissions program at the University of Texas is lawful under the Equal Protection Clause. [Although] the University's new admissions policy was a direct result of Grutter, it is not identical to the policy this Court approved in that case. Instead, consistent with the State's legislative directive, the University continues to fill a significant majority of its class through the Top Ten Percent Plan (or Plan). Today, up to 75 percent of the places in the freshman class are filled through the Plan. As a practical matter, this 75 percent cap, which has now been fixed by statute, means that, while the Plan continues to be referenced as a "Top Ten Percent Plan," a student actually needs to finish in the top seven or eight percent of his or her class in order to be admitted under this category.

The University did adopt an approach similar to the one in *Grutter* for the remaining 25 percent or so of the incoming class. This portion of the class continues to be admitted based on a combination of their AI and PAI scores. Now, however, race is given weight as a sub-factor within the Personal Achievement Index.

[Therefore], although admissions officers can consider race as a positive feature of a minority student's application, there is no dispute that race is but a "factor of a factor of a factor" in the holistic-review calculus.

[The] University's program is *sui generis*. Unlike other approaches to college admissions considered by this Court, it combines holistic review with a percentage plan. This approach gave rise to an unusual consequence in this case: The component of the University's admissions policy that had the largest impact on petitioner's chances of admission was not the school's consideration of race under its holistic-review process but rather the Top Ten Percent Plan. Because petitioner did not graduate in the top 10 percent of her high school class, she was categorically ineligible for more than three-fourths of the slots in the incoming freshman class. It seems quite plausible, then, to think that petitioner would have had a better chance of being admitted to the University if the school used race-conscious holistic review to select its entire incoming class, as was the case in Grutter.

Despite the Top Ten Percent Plan's outsized effect on petitioner's chances of admission, she has not challenged it. For that reason, throughout this litigation, the Top Ten Percent Plan has been taken, somewhat artificially, as a given premise.

Petitioner's acceptance of the Top Ten Percent Plan complicates this Court's review. In particular, it has led to a record that is almost devoid of information about the students who secured admission to the University through the Plan. The Court thus cannot know how students admitted solely based on their class rank differ in their contribution to diversity from students admitted through holistic review.

[The] fact that this case has been litigated on a somewhat artificial basis, furthermore, may limit its value for prospective guidance. The Texas Legislature, in enacting the Top Ten Percent Plan, cannot much be criticized, for it was responding to Hopwood, which at the time was binding law in the State of Texas. That legislative response, in turn, circumscribed the University's discretion in crafting its admissions policy.

[That] does not diminish, however, the University's continuing obligation to satisfy the burden of strict scrutiny in light of changing circumstances. The University engages in periodic reassessment of the constitutionality, and efficacy, of its admissions program. Going forward, that assessment must be undertaken in light of the experience the school has accumulated and the data it has gathered since the adoption of its admissions plan.

As the University examines this data, it should remain mindful that diversity takes many forms. Formalistic racial classifications may sometimes fail to capture diversity in all of its dimensions and, when used in a divisive manner, could undermine the educational benefits the University values. Through regular evaluation of data and consideration of student experience, the University must tailor its approach in light of changing circumstances, ensuring that race plays no greater role than is necessary to meet its compelling interest. The University's examination of the data it has acquired in the years since petitioner's application, for these reasons, must proceed with full respect for the constraints imposed by the Equal Protection Clause. The type of data collected, and the manner in which it is considered, will have a significant bearing on how the University must shape its admissions policy to satisfy strict scrutiny in the years to come.

[As] this Court's cases have made clear, however, the compelling interest that justifies consideration of race in college admissions is not an interest in enrolling a certain number of minority students. Rather, a university may institute a race-conscious admissions program as a means of obtaining "the educational benefits that flow from student body diversity." Fisher I, see also Grutter. As this Court has said, enrolling a diverse student body "promotes cross-racial understanding, helps to break down racial stereotypes, and enables students to better understand persons of different races." Id. Equally important, "student body diversity promotes learning outcomes, and better prepares students for an increasingly diverse workforce and society." *Id.*

Increasing minority enrollment may be instrumental to these educational benefits, but it is not [a] goal that can or should be reduced to pure numbers. Indeed, since the University is prohibited from seeking a particular number or quota of minority students, it cannot be faulted for failing to specify the particular level of minority enrollment at which it believes the educational benefits of diversity will be obtained.

On the other hand, asserting an interest in the educational benefits of diversity writ large is insufficient. A university's goals cannot be elusory or amorphous—they must be sufficiently measurable to permit judicial scrutiny of the policies adopted to reach them.

The record reveals that in first setting forth its current admissions policy, the University articulated concrete and precise goals. [The] University identifies the educational values it seeks to realize through its admissions process: the destruction of stereotypes, the " 'promot[ion of] cross-racial understanding,' " the preparation of a student body " 'for an increasingly diverse workforce and society,' " and the " 'cultivat[ion of] a set of leaders with legitimacy in the eyes of the citizenry.' " Later in the proposal, the University explains that it strives to provide an "academic environment" that offers a "robust exchange of ideas, exposure to differing cultures, preparation for the challenges of an increasingly diverse workforce, and acquisition of competencies required of future leaders." All of these objectives, as a general matter, mirror the "compelling interest" this Court has approved in its prior cases.

The University has provided in addition a "reasoned, principled explanation" for its decision to pursue these goals. The University's 39-page proposal was written following a year-long study, which concluded that "[t]he use of race-neutral policies and programs ha[d] not been successful" in "provid[ing] an educational setting that fosters cross-racial understanding, provid[ing] enlightened discussion and learning, [or] prepar[ing] students to function in an increasingly diverse workforce and society."

[A] university bears a heavy burden in showing that it had not obtained the educational benefits of diversity before it turned to a race-conscious plan. The record reveals, however, that, at the time of petitioner's application, the University could not be faulted on this score. [The] demographic data the University has submitted show consistent stagnation in terms of the percentage of minority students enrolling at the University from 1996 to 2002. In 1996, for example, 266 African-American freshmen enrolled, a total that constituted 4.1 percent of the incoming class. In 2003, the year Grutter was decided, 267 African-American students enrolled—again, 4.1 percent of the incoming class. The numbers for Hispanic and Asian-American students tell a similar story. Although demographics alone are by no means dispositive, they do have some value as a gauge of the University's ability to enroll students who can offer underrepresented perspectives.

In addition to this broad demographic data, the University put forward evidence that minority students admitted under the Hopwood regime experienced feelings of loneliness and isolation.

This anecdotal evidence is, in turn, bolstered by further, more nuanced quantitative data. In 2002, 52 percent of undergraduate classes with at least five students had no African-American students enrolled in them, and 27 percent had only one African-American student. In other words, only 21 percent of undergraduate classes with five or more students in them had more than one African-American student enrolled. Twelve percent of these classes had no Hispanic students, as compared to 10 percent in 1996.

[Petitioner] argues that considering race was not necessary because such consideration has had only a " 'minimal impact' in advancing the [University's] compelling interest." [It] is not a failure of narrow tailoring for the impact of racial consideration to be minor. The fact that race consciousness played a role in only a small portion of admissions decisions should be a hallmark of narrow tailoring, not evidence of unconstitutionality.

[Petitioner] suggests that the University could intensify its outreach efforts to African-American and Hispanic applicants. But the University submitted extensive evidence of the many ways in which it already had intensified its outreach efforts to those students. The University has created three new scholarship programs, opened new regional admissions centers, increased its recruitment budget by half-a-million dollars, and organized over 1,000 recruitment events. Perhaps more significantly, in the wake of Hopwood, the University spent seven years attempting to achieve its compelling interest using race-neutral holistic review. None of these efforts succeeded, and petitioner fails to offer any meaningful way in which the University could have improved upon them at the time of her application.

Petitioner also suggests altering the weight given to academic and socioeconomic factors in the University's admissions calculus. This proposal ignores the fact that the University tried, and failed, to increase diversity through enhanced consideration of socioeconomic and other factors. And it further ignores this Court's precedent making clear that the Equal Protection Clause does not force universities to choose between a diverse student body and a reputation for academic excellence. Grutter.

Petitioner's final suggestion is to uncap the Top Ten Percent Plan, and admit more—if not all—the University's students through a percentage plan. As an initial matter, petitioner overlooks the fact that the Top Ten Percent Plan, though facially neutral, cannot be understood apart from its basic purpose, which is to boost minority enrollment.

[Even] if, as a matter of raw numbers, minority enrollment would increase under such a regime, petitioner would be hard-pressed to find convincing support for the proposition that college admissions would be improved if they were a function of class rank alone. That approach would sacrifice all other aspects of diversity in pursuit of enrolling a higher number of minority students. [Class] rank is a single metric, and like any single metric, it will capture certain types of people and miss others. This does not imply that students admitted through holistic review are necessarily more capable or more desirable than those admitted through the Top Ten Percent Plan. It merely reflects the fact that privileging one characteristic above all others does not lead to a diverse student body. Indeed, to compel universities to admit students based on class rank alone is in deep tension with the goal of educational diversity as this Court's cases have defined it.

■ JUSTICE ALITO, with whom THE CHIEF JUSTICE and JUSTICE THOMAS join, dissenting.

Something strange has happened since our prior decision in this case. In that decision, we held that strict scrutiny requires the University of Texas at Austin (UT or University) to show that its use of race and ethnicity in making admissions decisions serves compelling interests and that its plan is narrowly tailored to achieve those ends. [On] remand, UT failed to do what our prior decision demanded. The University has still not identified with any degree of specificity the interests that its use of race and ethnicity is supposed to serve. Its primary argument is that merely invoking "the educational benefits of diversity" is sufficient and that it need not identify any metric that would allow a court to determine whether its plan is needed to serve, or is actually serving, those interests. This is nothing less than the plea for deference that we emphatically rejected in our prior decision. Today, however, the Court inexplicably grants that request.

[It] is important to understand what is and what is not at stake in this case. *What is not at stake* is whether UT or any other university may adopt an admissions plan that results in a student body with a broad representation of students from all racial and ethnic groups.

[*What is at stake*] is whether university administrators may justify systematic racial discrimination simply by asserting that such discrimination is necessary to achieve "the educational benefits of diversity," without explaining—much less proving—why the discrimination is needed or how the discriminatory plan is well crafted to serve its objectives. Even though UT has never provided any coherent explanation for its asserted need to discriminate on the basis of race, and even though UT's position relies on a series of unsupported and noxious racial assumptions, the majority concludes that UT has met its heavy burden. This conclusion is remarkable—and remarkably wrong.

SECTION 3. SEX DISCRIMINATION

Page 785. Add after Note 6, *Discrimination against unmarried fathers*:

In **Sessions v. Morales-Santana**, 579 U.S. ___, 137 S.Ct. 1678 (2017), Justice GINSBURG, writing for six justices, applied intermediate scrutiny to invalidate, under the equal protection principle implicit in the Fifth Amendment, a federal statutory scheme that, as applicable to the respondent, allowed an unwed U.S.-citizen mother to transmit citizenship to her child born abroad if she has lived continuously in the United States for just one year prior to the child's birth, while requiring ten years' physical presence in the United States prior to the child's birth, at least five of which were after attaining age eighteen, for unwed U.S.-citizen fathers and for married parents. The scheme traced to amendments to the Immigration and Nationality Act enacted in 1940 and 1952. Justice Ginsburg wrote: "History reveals what lurks behind § 1409. [During] this era, two once habitual, but now untenable, assumptions pervaded our Nation's citizenship laws and underpinned judicial and administrative rulings: In marriage, husband is dominant, wife subordinate; unwed mother is the natural and sole guardian of a non-marital child. [For] unwed parents, the father-controls tradition never held sway. Instead, the mother was regarded as the child's natural and sole guardian. [In] the 1940 Act, Congress discarded the father-controls assumption concerning married parents, but codified the mother-as-sole-guardian perception regarding unmarried parents. [Concern] about the attachment of foreign-born children to the United States explains the treatment of unwed citizen fathers, who, according to the familiar stereotype, would care little about, and have scant contact with, their nonmarital children. For unwed citizen mothers, however, there was no need for a prolonged residency prophylactic: The alien father, who might transmit foreign ways, was presumptively out of the picture. [Overbroad] generalizations of that order, the Court has come to comprehend, have a constraining impact, descriptive though they may be of the way many people still order their lives. Laws according or denying benefits in reliance on '[s]tereotypes about women's domestic roles,' the Court has observed, may 'creat[e] a self-fulfilling cycle of discrimination that force[s] women to continue to assume the role of primary family caregiver.' Nevada Dept. of Human Resources v. Hibbs. Correspondingly, such laws may disserve men who exercise responsibility for raising their children. In light of the equal protection jurisprudence this Court has developed, [the law's] discrete duration-of-residence requirements for unwed mothers and fathers who have accepted parental responsibility is stunningly anachronistic."

Yet having struck down the disparity in treatment, the Court that held that the remedy was not to shorten the residency for fathers but to eliminate the favorable treatment of unwed mothers. Justice Ginsburg wrote: "The choice between these outcomes is governed by the legislature's intent, as revealed by the statute at hand. Ordinarily, we have reiterated, 'extension, rather than nullification, is the proper course.' [Here,] however, the discriminatory exception consists of favorable treatment for a discrete group (a shorter physical-presence requirement for unwed U.S.-citizen mothers giving birth abroad). [The] residual policy here, the longer physical-presence requirement, [evidences] Congress' recognition of the importance of residence in this country as the talisman of dedicated attachment. And the potential for disruption of the statutory scheme is large. For if § 1409(c)'s one-year dispensation were extended to unwed citizen fathers, would it not be irrational to retain the longer term when the U.S.-citizen parent is married? Disadvantageous treatment of marital children in comparison to nonmarital children is scarcely a purpose one can sensibly attribute to Congress. [Put] to the choice, Congress, we believe, would have abrogated § 1409(c)'s exception, preferring preservation of the general rule." Justice THOMAS, joined by Justice Alito, concurred only in the judgment, stating that, in light of the remedy, the constitutional issue should not have been reached. Justice Gorsuch did not participate.

Note that this is the first instance in which the Court, having found unconstitutional gender-stereotyping favoring women, chose to remedy the inequality by levelling down rather than levelling up. Is this remedy the correct one? If the Court may not strip citizenship retroactively from children born abroad to unwed U.S.-citizen mothers who had already benefited from the favorable U.S.-residency requirement, doesn't this result leave intact unequal treatment of existing children born abroad to similarly-situated unwed U.S.-citizen fathers?

SECTION 5. THE "FUNDAMENTAL INTERESTS" BRANCH OF EQUAL PROTECTION

Page 818. Add after Reynolds v. Sims:

In **Evenwel v. Abbott**, 578 U.S. ___, 136 S.Ct. 1120 (2016), a group of Texas voters argued that the principle of one person, one vote should be understood as requiring one voter, one-vote. They challenged Texas's population-based districting on the ground that it produces unequal districts when measured by voter-eligible population. The Court rejected the claim that only the population of eligible voters could be used in determining districts. Justice GINSBURG wrote: "We hold, based on constitutional history, this Court's decisions, and longstanding practice, that a State may draw its legislative districts based on total population. [James] Madison explained in the Federalist Papers, 'that as the aggregate number of representatives allotted to the several states, is to be . . . founded on the aggregate number of inhabitants; so, the right of choosing this allotted number in each state, is to be exercised by such part of the inhabitants, as the state itself may designate.' The Federalist No. 54. In other words, the basis of *representation* in the House was to include all inhabitants—although slaves were counted as only three-fifths of a person—even though States remained free to deny many of those inhabitants the right to participate in the selection of their representatives. [The] Framers of the Fourteenth Amendment considered at length the possibility of allocating House seats to States on the basis of voter population. [Supporters] of apportionment based on voter population employed the same voter-equality reasoning that appellants now echo. [Voter-based] apportionment proponents encountered fierce resistance from proponents of total-population apportionment. Much of the opposition was grounded in the principle of representational equality. [The] product of these debates was § 2 of the Fourteenth Amendment, which retained total population as the congressional apportionment base. See U.S. Const., Amdt. 14, § 2 ("Representatives shall be apportioned among the several States according to their respective numbers, counting the whole number of persons in each State, excluding Indians not taxed."). Appellants ask us to find in the Fourteenth Amendment's Equal Protection Clause a rule inconsistent with this "theory of the Constitution." But [this] theory underlies not just the method of allocating House seats to States; it applies as well to the method of apportioning legislative seats within States. [Reynolds] involved features of the federal electoral system that contravene the principles of both voter *and* representational equality to favor interests that have no relevance outside the federal context. Senate seats were allocated to States on an equal basis to respect state sovereignty and increase the odds that the smaller States would ratify the Constitution. [The] Framers' answer to the apportionment question in the congressional context therefore undermines appellants' contention that districts must be based on voter population.

Justice THOMAS concurred but wrote separately to say that "this Court has never provided a sound basis for the one-person, one-vote principle." Justice ALITO also concurred, joined by Justice Thomas, to reject the "meretricious argument" that "the one-person, one-vote principle requires districts that are equal in total population. [First], the allocation of congressional representation sheds little light on the question [because] that allocation plainly violates one person, one vote. This is obviously true with respect to the Senate. [Second], Reynolds v. Sims squarely rejected the argument that the Constitution's allocation of congressional representation establishes the test for the constitutionality of a state legislative districting plan. [Third], reliance on the Constitution's allocation of congressional representation is profoundly ahistorical. When the formula for allocating House seats was first devised in 1787 and reconsidered at the time of the adoption of the Fourteenth Amendment in 1868, the overwhelming concern was far removed from any abstract theory about the nature of representation. Instead, the dominant consideration was the distribution of political power among the States."

Page 823. Add after Note 2, *What is the harm in partisan gerrymandering?*

In **Gill v. Whitford**, 585 U.S. ___, 137 S.Ct. 2268 (2018), Democratic voters in Wisconsin alleged that a state redistricting plan harmed their party's ability to convert Democratic votes into Democratic seats in the legislature through "cracking" Democratic voters among different districts in which those voters fail to achieve electoral majorities and "packing" other Democratic voters in a few districts in which Democratic candidates win by large margins. To address justiciability, they offered the theory of an "efficiency gap" that compares each party's respective "wasted" votes—*i.e.*, votes cast for a losing candidate or for a winning candidate in excess of what that candidate needs to win—across all legislative districts. In an opinion by Chief Justice ROBERTS, the Court held that the voters lacked standing because they had not demonstrated particularized injury: "To the extent the plaintiffs' alleged harm is the dilution of their votes, that injury is district specific. [The] boundaries of the district, and the composition of its voters, determine whether and to what extent a particular voter is packed or cracked. [Remedying] the individual voter's harm, therefore, does not necessarily require restructuring all of the State's legislative districts. It requires revising only such districts as are necessary to reshape the voter's district—so that the voter may be unpacked or uncracked, as the case may be. [In] cases where a plaintiff fails to demonstrate Article III standing, we usually direct the dismissal of the plaintiff's claims. This is not the usual case. It concerns an unsettled kind of claim this Court has not agreed upon, the contours and justiciability of which are unresolved. Under the circumstances, [we] decline to direct dismissal." In concurrence, Justice KAGAN, joined by Justices Ginsburg, Breyer, and Sotomayor, agreed with the remand for lack of standing, but introduced an "associational theory" of harm based on Justice Kennedy's concurrence in Vieth v. Jubilirer to show

how "partisan gerrymanders may infringe the First Amendment rights of association held by parties, other political organizations, and their members." Such an associational claim, she wrote, "would occasion a different standing inquiry" because "the gerrymander has burdened the ability of like-minded people across the State to affiliate in a political party and carry out that organization's activities and objects." She acknowledged that partisan gerrymandering was an old practice, but explained that "technology makes today's gerrymandering altogether different from the crude linedrawing of the past. New redistricting software enables pinpoint precision in designing districts. With such tools, mapmakers can capture every last bit of partisan advantage, while still meeting traditional districting requirements (compactness, contiguity, and the like). Gerrymanders have thus become ever more extreme and durable, insulating officeholders against all but the most titanic shifts in the political tides. [Courts] have a critical role to play in curbing partisan gerrymandering. [This Court] will again be called on to redress extreme partisan gerrymanders. I am hopeful we will then step up to our responsibility to vindicate the Constitution against a contrary law."

Justice Kagan's concurrence was widely read as an appeal to Justice Kennedy to adopt his Vieth theory in a future case. But Justice Kennedy resigned just ten days after the opinion appeared. What does that say about Justice Kagan's appeal, if that is what it was?

CHAPTER 12

FREEDOM OF SPEECH—MODES OF REGULATION AND STANDARDS OF REVIEW

SECTION 1. CONTENT-BASED AND CONTENT-NEUTRAL REGULATIONS

Page 1213. Add new Note after Nude Dancing:

SPEECH VERSUS CONDUCT IN PRICING

In **Expressions Hair Design v. Schneiderman**, 581 U.S. ___, 137 S.Ct. 1144 (2017), the Court considered a free-speech challenge to New York State law that prohibited merchants from telling customers that they must pay a surcharge on credit-card transactions. In an opinion by Chief Justice ROBERTS, the Court held that the law regulated speech, not conduct, as the Second Circuit had held: "[A] typical price regulation[—for] example, a law requiring all New York delis to charge $10 for their sandwiches—would simply regulate the amount that a store could collect. In other words, it would regulate the sandwich seller's conduct. To be sure, in order to actually collect that money, a store would likely have to put '$10' on its menus or have its employees tell customers that price. Those written or oral communications would be speech, and the law—by determining the amount charged—would indirectly dictate the content of that speech. But the law's effect on speech would be only incidental to its primary effect on conduct. [This law] is different. The law tells merchants nothing about the amount they are allowed to collect from a cash or credit card payer. Sellers are free to charge $10 for cash and $9.70, $10, $10.30, or any other amount for credit. What the law does regulate is how sellers may communicate their prices. A merchant who wants to charge $10 for cash and $10.30 for credit may not convey that price any way he pleases. He is not free to say '$10, with a 3% credit card surcharge' or '$10, plus $0.30 for credit' because both of those displays identify a single sticker price—$10—that is less than the amount credit card users will be charged. Instead, if the merchant wishes to post a single sticker price, he must display $10.30 as his sticker price. Accordingly, [we] cannot accept [the] conclusion that [the law] is nothing more than a mine-run price regulation. In regulating the communication of prices rather than prices themselves, [the law] regulates speech. [The] parties dispute whether [the law] is a valid commercial speech regulation under Central Hudson Gas & Elec. Corp. v. Public Serv. Comm'n of N. Y., and whether the law can be upheld as a valid disclosure requirement under Zauderer v. Office of Disciplinary Counsel of Supreme Court of Ohio. [We] decline to consider those questions in the first instance. Instead, we remand for the Court of Appeals to analyze [the law] as a speech regulation." Does Chief Justice

Roberts's opinion telegraph an answer to the question whether the credit-card regulation is commercial speech? And if so, whether the regulation is valid?

SECTION 2. GOVERNMENT'S POWER TO LIMIT SPEECH AS QUASI-PRIVATE ACTOR

Page 1284. Add after Note 13, *Rights of access to public property*:

14. *Polling place.* In **Minnesota Voters Alliance v. Mansky**, 585 U.S. ___, 138 S.Ct. 1876 (2018), the Court struck down a Minnesota law prohibiting individuals from wearing a "political badge, political button, or other political insignia" inside a polling place on Election Day. Chief Justice ROBERTS wrote for the 7–2 Court: "Today, all 50 States and the District of Columbia have laws curbing various forms of speech in and around polling places on Election Day. [The Minnesota] ban applies only in a specific location: the interior of a polling place. [A] polling place in Minnesota qualifies as a nonpublic forum. It is, at least on Election Day, government-controlled property set aside for the sole purpose of voting. [The] question accordingly is whether Minnesota's ban on political apparel is reasonable in light of the purpose served by the forum: voting. [In] light of the special purpose of the polling place itself, Minnesota may choose to prohibit certain apparel there because of the message it conveys, so that voters may focus on the important decisions immediately at hand. [Although] there is no requirement of narrow tailoring in a nonpublic forum, the State must be able to articulate some sensible basis for distinguishing what may come in from what must stay out. Here, the unmoored use of the term 'political' in the Minnesota law, combined with haphazard interpretations the State has provided in official guidance and representations to this Court, cause Minnesota's restriction to fail even this forgiving test.

"[The] State interprets the ban to proscribe 'only words and symbols that an objectively reasonable observer would perceive as conveying a message about the electoral choices at issue in [the] polling place.' At the same time, the State argues that the category of 'political' apparel is *not* limited to campaign apparel. [Far] from clarifying the indeterminate scope of the political apparel provision, the State's 'electoral choices' construction introduces confusing line-drawing problems. [The] State points to the 2010 Election Day Policy—which it continues to hold out as authoritative guidance regarding implementation of the statute. The first three examples in the Policy are clear enough: items displaying the name of a political party, items displaying the name of a candidate, and items demonstrating 'support of or opposition to a ballot question.' But the next example—'[i]ssue oriented material designed to influence or impact voting,'—raises more questions than it answers. What qualifies as an 'issue'? The answer, as far as we can tell from the State's briefing and argument, is any subject on which a political candidate or party has taken a stance. For instance, the Election Day Policy specifically notes that the 'Please I.D. Me' buttons are prohibited. But a voter identification requirement was not on the ballot in 2010, so a Minnesotan would have had no explicit 'electoral choice' to make in that respect. The buttons were nonetheless covered, the State tells us, because the Republican candidates for Governor and Secretary of State had staked out positions on whether photo identification should be required.

"A rule whose fair enforcement requires an election judge to maintain a mental index of the platforms and positions of every candidate and party on the ballot is not reasonable. Candidates for statewide and federal office and major political parties can be expected to take positions on a wide array of subjects of local and national import. [The] next broad category in the Election Day Policy—any item 'promoting a group with recognizable political views,'—makes matters worse. [The] American Civil Liberties Union, the AARP, the World Wildlife Fund, and Ben & Jerry's all have stated positions on matters of public concern.

"[That] is not to say that Minnesota has set upon an impossible task. Other States have laws proscribing displays (including apparel) in more lucid terms. We do not suggest that such provisions set the outer limit of what a State may proscribe, and do not pass on the constitutionality of laws that are not before us. But we do hold that if a State wishes to set its polling places apart as areas free of partisan discord, it must employ a more discernible approach than the one Minnesota has offered here."

In dissent, Justice SOTOMAYOR, joined by Justice Breyer, wrote that she would have certified the case to the Minnesota Supreme Court for a definitive interpretation of the political apparel ban, likely obviating "the hypothetical line-drawing problems that form the basis of the Court's decision today."

Note that the Court applied the most lenient level of forum analysis—the deferential scrutiny applicable to a nonpublic forum—but still struck down the law as an unconstitutional restriction of speech. What accounts for that decision? In another polling place speech case, Burson v. Freeman (19th ed., p. 1169), the plurality applied strict scrutiny to a signage ban outside the polling place but still upheld the law. Can the decisions be reconciled?

Page 1317. Add new Note after Note 4, _Pickering, Connick, and school athletic associations_:

5.   _Targeting error and intent._ In **Heffernan v. City of Paterson**, 578 U.S. ___, 136 S.Ct. 1412 (2016), the Court addressed a situation in which the government employer targeted an employee's speech based on a mistake of fact. A police officer was targeted for supporting a mayoral candidate, but in fact he was not supporting the candidate and had merely picked up one of the candidate's signs for his mother. Justice BREYER wrote the opinion for the Court, holding that the First Amendment covered the situation: "In this case a government official demoted an employee because the official believed, but _incorrectly_ believed, that the employee had supported a particular candidate for mayor. [When] an employer demotes an employee out of a desire to prevent the employee from engaging in political activity that the First Amendment protects, the employee is entitled to challenge that unlawful action under the First Amendment—[even] if, as here, the employer makes a factual mistake about the employee's behavior. [A] rule of law finding liability in these circumstances tracks the language of the First

Amendment more closely than would a contrary rule. Unlike, say, the Fourth Amendment, which begins by speaking of the 'right of the people to be secure in their persons, houses, papers, and effects,' the First Amendment begins by focusing upon the activity of the Government. [We] also consider relevant the constitutional implications of a rule that imposes liability. The constitutional harm at issue in the ordinary case consists in large part of discouraging employees—both the employee discharged (or demoted) and his or her colleagues—from engaging in protected activities. The discharge of one tells the others that they engage in protected activity at their peril. [The] employer's factual mistake does not diminish the risk of causing precisely that same harm."

Justice THOMAS, joined by Justice Alito, dissented, reasoning that Section 1983 "does not provide a cause of action to plaintiffs whose constitutional rights have not been violated."

Page 1346. Add new Note 8:

8. *Viewpoint and Trademark.*

Matal v. Tam

581 U.S. ___, 137 S.Ct. 1744, 198 L.Ed.2d 366 (2017).

[Simon Tam, lead singer of dance-rock band called "The Slants," chose the name to "reclaim" the anti-Asian slur. The members of the ban are Asian-Americans. Tam sought federal registration of the mark "THE SLANTS" from the Patent and Trademark Office (PTO), which denied the application under a Lanham Act provision prohibiting the registration of trademarks that may "disparage . . . or bring . . . into contemp[t] or disrepute" any "persons, living or dead." 15 U.S.C. § 1052(a).]

■ JUSTICE ALITO announced the judgment of the Court and delivered the opinion of the Court with respect to Parts I, II, and III-A, and an opinion with respect to Parts III-B, III-C, and IV, in which THE CHIEF JUSTICE, JUSTICE THOMAS, and JUSTICE BREYER join:

[We] now hold that this provision violates the Free Speech Clause of the First Amendment. It offends a bedrock First Amendment principle: Speech may not be banned on the ground that it expresses ideas that offend.

I. [Federal] law does not create trademarks. Trademarks and their precursors have ancient origins, and trademarks were protected at common law and in equity at the time of the founding. [For] most of the 19th century, trademark protection was the province of the States. [Under] the Lanham Act, [there] are now more than two million marks that have active federal certificates of registration. [Without] federal registration, a valid trademark may still be used in commerce. And an unregistered trademark can be enforced against would-be infringers in several ways. Most important, even if a trademark is not federally registered, it may still be enforceable under § 43(a) of the Lanham Act, which creates a federal cause of action for trademark infringement. And an unregistered trademark can be enforced under state common law, or if it has been registered in a State, under that State's registration system. Federal registration, however, [(1) serves] as constructive notice of the registrant's claim of ownership of the mark; (2) is prima facie evidence of the validity of the registered mark and of the registration of the mark, of the owner's ownership of the mark, and of the owner's exclusive right to use the registered mark in commerce on or in connection with the goods or services specified in the certificate; and (3) can make a mark incontestable once a mark has been registered for five years.

[At] issue in this case is [what] we will call "the disparagement clause." [When] deciding whether a trademark is disparaging, an examiner at the PTO generally applies a two-part test. The examiner first considers the likely meaning of the matter in question. ["If] that meaning is found to refer to identifiable persons, institutions, beliefs or national symbols," the examiner moves to the second step, asking "whether that meaning may be disparaging to a substantial composite of the referenced group." If the examiner finds that a "substantial composite, although not necessarily a majority, of the referenced group would find the proposed mark . . . to be disparaging in the context of contemporary attitudes," a prima facie case of disparagement is made out, and the burden shifts to the applicant to prove that the trademark is not disparaging. What is more, the PTO has specified that "[t]he fact that an applicant may be a member of that group or has good intentions underlying its use of a term does not obviate the fact that a substantial composite of the referenced group would find the term objectionable."

II. [Before] reaching the question whether the disparagement clause violates the First Amendment, we consider Tam's argument that the clause does not reach marks that disparage racial or ethnic groups [because] racial and ethnic groups are neither natural nor "juristic" persons. Tam's argument is refuted by the plain terms of the disparagement clause. [A] mark that disparages a "substantial" percentage of the members of a racial or ethnic group necessarily disparages many "persons," namely, members of that group.

III. [At] the outset, we must consider three arguments that would either eliminate any First Amendment protection or result in highly permissive rational-basis review. Specifically, the Government contends (1) that trademarks are government speech, not private speech, (2) that trademarks are a form of government subsidy, and (3) that the constitutionality of the disparagement clause should be tested under a new "government-program" doctrine.

A. [Our] cases recognize that "the Free Speech Clause . . . does not regulate government speech." Pleasant Grove City v. Summum. [But] while the government-speech doctrine is important—indeed, essential—it is a doctrine that is susceptible to dangerous misuse. If private speech could be passed off as government speech by simply affixing a government seal of approval, government could silence or muffle the expression of disfavored.

[At] issue here is the content of trademarks that are registered by the PTO. [The] Federal Government does not dream up these marks, and it does not edit marks submitted for registration. Except as required by the statute involved here, an examiner may not reject a mark based on the viewpoint that it appears to express. Thus, unless that section is thought to apply, [registration] is mandatory. [If] an examiner finds that a mark is eligible for placement on the principal register, that decision is not reviewed by any higher official unless the registration is challenged. Moreover, once a mark is registered, the PTO is not authorized to remove it from the register. [In] light of all this, it is far-fetched to suggest that the content of a registered mark is government speech. If the federal registration of a trademark makes the mark government speech, the Federal Government is babbling prodigiously and incoherently.

[The] case on which the Government relies most heavily, Walker, [likely] marks the outer bounds of the government-speech doctrine. Holding that the messages on Texas specialty license plates are government speech, the Walker Court cited three factors distilled from Summum. First, license plates have long been used by the States to convey state messages. Second, license plates "are often closely identified in the public mind" with the State, since they are manufactured and owned by the State, generally designed by the State, and serve as a form of "government ID." Third, Texas "maintain[ed] direct control over the messages conveyed on its specialty plates." [None] of these factors are present in this case.

[If] the registration of trademarks constituted government speech, other systems of government registration could easily be characterized in the same way. [If] federal registration makes a trademark government speech and thus eliminates all First Amendment protection, would the registration of the copyright for a book produce a similar transformation? The Government attempts to distinguish copyright on the ground that it is "the engine of free expression," but as this case illustrates, trademarks often have an expressive content. Trademarks are private, not government, speech.

B. We next address the Government's argument that this case is governed by cases in which this Court has upheld the constitutionality of government programs that subsidized speech expressing a particular viewpoint. These cases implicate a notoriously tricky question of constitutional law. [Unlike] the present case, the decisions on which the Government relies all involved cash subsidies or their equivalent. In Rust v. Sullivan, a federal law provided funds to private parties for family planning services. In National Endowment for Arts v. Finley, cash grants were awarded to artists. And federal funding for public libraries was at issue in United States v. American Library Assn., Inc. [Th]e federal registration of a trademark is nothing like the programs at issue in these cases. The PTO does not pay money to parties seeking registration of a mark.

C. [Finally,] the Government urges us to sustain the disparagement clause under a new doctrine that would apply to "government-program" cases. [But] those cases occupy a special area of First Amendment case law, and they are far removed from the registration of trademarks.

[Potentially] more analogous are cases in which a unit of government creates a limited public forum for private speech. When government creates such a forum, in either a literal or "metaphysical" sense, see Rosenberger, some content- and speaker-based restrictions may be allowed. However, even in such cases, what we have termed "viewpoint discrimination" is forbidden.

Our cases use the term "viewpoint" discrimination in a broad sense, and in that sense, the disparagement clause discriminates on the bases of "viewpoint." To be sure, the clause evenhandedly prohibits disparagement of all groups. It applies equally to marks that damn Democrats and Republicans, capitalists and socialists, and those arrayed on both sides of every possible issue. It denies registration to any mark that is offensive to a substantial percentage of the members of any group. But in the sense relevant here, that is viewpoint discrimination: Giving offense is a viewpoint.

IV. [The parties dispute] whether trademarks are commercial speech and are thus subject to the relaxed scrutiny outlined in *Central Hudson*. We need not resolve this debate [because] the disparagement clause cannot withstand even *Central Hudson* review.

It is claimed that the disparagement clause serves two interests. The first is [that] Government has an interest in preventing speech expressing ideas that offend. [That] idea strikes at the heart of the First Amendment. Speech that demeans on the basis of race, ethnicity, gender, religion, age, disability, or any other similar ground is hateful; but the proudest boast of our free speech jurisprudence is that we protect the freedom to express "the thought that we hate."

The second interest asserted is protecting the orderly flow of commerce. [A] simple answer [is] that the disparagement clause is not "narrowly drawn" to drive out trademarks that support invidious discrimination. [It] applies to trademarks like the following: "Down with racists," "Down with sexists," "Down with homophobes." It is not an anti-discrimination clause; it is a happy-talk clause.

[There] is also a deeper problem with the argument that commercial speech may be cleansed of any expression likely to cause offense. The commercial market is well stocked with merchandise that disparages prominent figures and groups, and the line between commercial and non-commercial speech is not always clear. [If] affixing the commercial label permits the suppression of any speech that may lead to political or social "volatility," free speech would be endangered.

■ JUSTICE KENNEDY, with whom JUSTICE GINSBURG, JUSTICE SOTOMAYOR, and JUSTICE KAGAN join, concurring in part and concurring in the judgment.

[This] separate writing explains in greater detail why the First Amendment's protections against viewpoint discrimination apply to the trademark here. It submits further that the viewpoint discrimination rationale renders unnecessary any extended treatment of other questions raised by the parties.

[In] the instant case, the disparagement clause [identifies] the relevant subject as "persons, living or dead, institutions, beliefs, or national symbols." 15 U.S.C. § 1052(a). Within that category, an applicant may register a positive or benign mark but not a derogatory one. The law thus reflects the Government's disapproval of a subset of messages it finds offensive. This is the essence of viewpoint discrimination.

[To] prohibit all sides from criticizing their opponents makes a law more viewpoint based, not less so. The logic of the Government's rule is that a law would be viewpoint neutral even if it provided that public officials could be praised but not condemned. The First Amendment's viewpoint neutrality principle protects more than the right to identify with a particular side. It protects the right to create and present arguments for particular positions in particular ways, as the speaker chooses. By mandating positivity, the law here might silence dissent and distort the marketplace of ideas.

[The] Court has suggested that viewpoint discrimination occurs when the government intends to suppress a speaker's beliefs, but viewpoint discrimination need not take that form in every instance. The danger of viewpoint discrimination is that the government is attempting to remove certain ideas or perspectives from a broader debate. That danger is all the greater if the ideas or perspectives are ones a particular audience might think offensive, at least at first hearing. An initial reaction may prompt further reflection, leading to a more reasoned, more tolerant position.

[To] the extent trademarks qualify as commercial speech, they are an example of why that term or category does not serve as a blanket exemption from the First Amendment's requirement of viewpoint neutrality. Justice Holmes' reference to the "free trade in ideas" and the "power of . . . thought to get itself accepted in the competition of the market," Abrams v. United States, (dissenting opinion), was a metaphor. In the realm of trademarks, the metaphorical marketplace of ideas becomes a tangible, powerful reality. Here that real marketplace exists as a matter of state law and our common-law tradition, quite without regard to the Federal Government. These marks make up part of the expression of everyday life. [To] permit viewpoint discrimination in this context is to permit Government censorship.

CHAPTER 13

BEYOND SPEAKING— COMPELLED SPEECH, ASSOCIATION, MONEY, AND THE MEDIA

SECTION 1. COMPELLED SPEECH: THE RIGHT *NOT* TO SPEAK

Page 1397. Add new Note 4:

4.   *Compelled disclosure by providers of professional services.*

National Institute of Family and Life Advocates v. Becerra

585 U.S. ___, 138 S.Ct. 2361 (2018).

[The California Reproductive Freedom, Accountability, Comprehensive Care, and Transparency Act (FACT Act) requires clinics that primarily serve pregnant women to notify patients that California provides free or low-cost services, including abortions, and to give them a phone number to call. Unlicensed clinics must notify patients that California has not licensed the clinics to provide medical services. The law was challenged by "crisis pregnancy centers" that aimed to discourage pregnant women from obtaining abortions.]

■ JUSTICE THOMAS delivered the opinion of the Court.

[The] licensed notice is a content-based regulation of speech. By compelling individuals to speak a particular message, such notices alter the content of their speech. Here, for example, licensed clinics must provide a government-drafted script about the availability of state-sponsored services, as well as contact information for how to obtain them. One of those services is abortion—the very practice that petitioners are devoted to opposing.

[Our] precedents have applied more deferential review to some laws that require professionals to disclose factual, noncontroversial information in their "commercial speech." See, e.g., Zauderer [19th ed., p. 1143]. [And under] our precedents, States may regulate professional conduct, even though that conduct incidentally involves speech. Casey [19th ed., p. 602]. But neither line of precedents is implicated here. [The] licensed notice at issue here is not an informed-consent requirement or any other regulation of professional conduct. The notice does not facilitate informed consent to a medical procedure. [The] licensed notice regulates speech as speech. Outside of the two contexts discussed above, [this] Court's precedents have long protected the First Amendment rights of professionals. [As] with other kinds of speech, regulating the content of professionals' speech "poses the inherent risk that the Government seeks not to advance a legitimate regulatory goal, but to suppress unpopular ideas or information." ["Professional speech"] is also a difficult category to define with precision. As defined by the courts of appeals, the professional-speech doctrine would cover a wide array of individuals—doctors, lawyers, nurses, physical therapists, truck drivers, bartenders, barbers, and many others. [But] that gives the States unfettered power to reduce a group's First Amendment rights by simply imposing a licensing requirement.

[California has not] identified a persuasive reason for treating professional speech as a unique category that is exempt from ordinary First Amendment principles. We do not foreclose the possibility that some such reason exists. We need not do so because the licensed notice cannot survive even intermediate scrutiny. California asserts a single interest to justify the licensed notice: providing low-income women with information about state-sponsored services. Assuming that this is a substantial state interest, the licensed notice is not sufficiently drawn to achieve it.

If California's goal is to educate low-income women about the services it provides, then the licensed notice is wildly underinclusive. The notice applies only to clinics that have a "primary purpose" of "providing family planning or pregnancy-related services" and that provide two of six categories of specific services. [Such] underinclusiveness raises serious doubts about whether the government is in fact pursuing the interest it invokes, rather than disfavoring a particular speaker or viewpoint. The FACT Act also excludes, without explanation, federal clinics and Family PACT providers from the licensed-notice requirement. [Further,] California could inform low-income women about its services [with] a public-information campaign.

[We] need not decide what type of state interest is sufficient to sustain a disclosure requirement like the unlicensed notice. [The] only justification that the California Legislature put forward was ensuring that "pregnant women in California know when they are getting medical care from licensed professionals." [Yet] California points to nothing suggesting that pregnant women do not already know that the covered facilities are staffed by unlicensed medical professionals. [California] already makes it a crime for individuals without a medical license to practice medicine. Even if California had presented a nonhypothetical justification for the unlicensed notice, the FACT Act unduly burdens protected speech. The unlicensed notice imposes a government-scripted, speaker-based disclosure requirement that is wholly disconnected from California's informational interest. [The] application of the unlicensed notice to advertisements demonstrates just how burdensome it is. [As] California conceded at oral argument, a billboard for an unlicensed facility that says "Choose Life" would have to surround that two-word statement with a 29-word statement from the government, in as many as 13 different languages. In this way, the unlicensed notice drowns out the facility's own message. More likely, the detail required by the unlicensed notice effectively rules out the possibility of having such a billboard in the first place.

[We] express no view on the legality of a similar disclosure requirement that is better supported or less burdensome.

■ JUSTICE KENNEDY, with whom the CHIEF JUSTICE, JUSTICE ALITO, and JUSTICE GORSUCH join, concurring.

[This] separate writing seeks to underscore that the apparent viewpoint discrimination here is a matter of serious constitutional concern. [This] law is a paradigmatic example of the serious threat presented when government seeks to impose its own message in the place of individual speech, thought, and expression. For here the State requires primarily pro-life pregnancy centers to promote the State's own preferred message advertising abortions. This compels individuals to contradict their most deeply held beliefs, beliefs grounded in basic philosophical, ethical, or religious precepts, or all of these. And the history of the Act's passage and its underinclusive application suggest a real possibility that these individuals were targeted because of their beliefs.

■ JUSTICE BREYER, with whom JUSTICE GINSBURG, JUSTICE SOTOMAYOR, and JUSTICE KAGAN join, dissenting.

[The] majority says it applies [heightened] scrutiny to the Act because the Act, in its view, is content based. [This] constitutional approach threatens to create serious problems. Because much, perhaps most, human behavior takes place through speech and because much, perhaps most, law regulates that speech in terms of its content, the majority's approach at the least threatens considerable litigation over the constitutional validity of much, perhaps most, government regulation. Virtually every disclosure law could be considered "content based," for virtually every disclosure law requires individuals "to speak a particular message." Thus, the majority's view, if taken literally, could radically change prior law, perhaps placing much securities law or consumer protection law at constitutional risk, depending on how broadly its exceptions are interpreted.

[The] majority, [perhaps] recognizing this problem, [says] that it does not "question the legality of health and safety warnings long considered permissible, or purely factual and uncontroversial disclosures about commercial products." But this generally phrased disclaimer would seem more likely to invite litigation than to provide needed limitation and clarification. The majority, for example, does not explain why the Act here, which is justified in part by health and safety considerations, does not fall within its "health" category.

[Precedent] does not require a test such as the majority's. [Historically,] the Court has been wary of claims that regulation of business activity, particularly health-related activity, violates the Constitution. Ever since this Court departed from the approach it set forth in Lochner [19th ed., p. 487], ordinary economic and social legislation has been thought to raise little constitutional concern. [The] Court has taken this same respectful approach to economic and social legislation when a First Amendment claim like the claim present here is at issue. Even during the Lochner era, when this Court struck down numerous economic regulations concerning industry, this Court was careful to defer to state legislative judgments concerning the medical profession. [In] the name of the First Amendment, the majority today treads into territory where the pre-New Deal, as well as the post-New Deal, Court refused to go.

In Casey [19th ed., p. 602], the Court [considered] a state law that required doctors to provide information to a woman deciding whether to proceed with an abortion. [The Court held that] the statute was constitutional. The joint opinion stated that the statutory requirements amounted to "reasonable measures to ensure an informed choice, one which might cause the woman to choose childbirth over abortion." [The] joint opinion specifically [concluded] that the statute did not violate the First Amendment. [If] a State can lawfully require a doctor to tell a woman seeking an abortion about adoption services, why should it not be able, as here, to require a medical counselor to tell a woman seeking prenatal care or other reproductive healthcare about childbirth and abortion services? As the question suggests, there is no convincing reason to distinguish between information about adoption and information about abortion in this context.

[With respect to the unlicensed clinics, there] is no basis for finding the State's interest "hypothetical." The legislature heard that information-related delays in qualified healthcare negatively affect women seeking to terminate their pregnancies as well as women carrying their pregnancies to term, with delays in qualified prenatal care causing life-long health problems for infants. [The] majority suggests that the Act is suspect because it covers some speakers but not others. [There] is no cause for such concern here. The Act does not, on its face, distinguish between facilities that favor pro-life and those that favor pro-choice points of view. Nor is there any convincing evidence before us or in the courts below that discrimination was the purpose or the effect of the statute. [Finally,] the majority concludes that the Act is overly burdensome. [But] these and similar claims are claims that the statute could be applied unconstitutionally, not that it is unconstitutional on its face.

SECTION 2. FREEDOM OF EXPRESSIVE ASSOCIATION

Page 1440. Add to the end of Note 1, *Compulsory fees to unions*:

In **Janus v. American Federation of State, County, and Municipal Employees, Council 31**, 585 U.S. ___, 138 S.Ct. 974 (2018), the Court in a 5–4 decision overruled the part of Abood that allowed collection of agency fees. Justice ALITO, who had written the opinions in Knox and Harris, wrote the opinion, joined by Chief Justice Roberts and Justices Kennedy, Thomas and Gorsuch: "Under Illinois law, public employees are forced to subsidize a union, even if they choose not to join and strongly object to the positions the union takes in collective bargaining and related activities. We conclude that this arrangement violates the free speech rights of nonmembers by compelling them to subsidize private speech on matters of substantial public concern.

"[Petitioner] in the present case contends that the Illinois law at issue should be subjected to strict scrutiny. The dissent, on the other hand, proposes that we apply what amounts to rational-basis review. [This] form of minimal scrutiny is foreign to our free-speech jurisprudence, and we reject it here. At the same time, we again find it unnecessary to decide the issue of strict scrutiny because the Illinois scheme cannot survive under even the more permissive standard applied in Knox and Harris.

"In Abood, the main defense of the agency-fee arrangement was that it served the State's interest in 'labor peace.' [We] assume that 'labor peace' [is] a compelling state interest, but Abood cited no evidence that the pandemonium it imagined would result if agency fees were not allowed.

"[The] federal employment experience is illustrative. Under federal law, a union chosen by majority vote is designated as the exclusive representative of all the employees, but federal law does not permit agency fees. Nevertheless, nearly a million federal employees—about 27% of the federal work force—are union members. [Likewise,] millions of public employees in the 28 States that have laws generally prohibiting agency fees are represented by unions that serve as the exclusive representatives of all the employees. Whatever may have been the case 41 years ago when Abood was handed down, it is now undeniable that 'labor peace' can readily be achieved through means significantly less restrictive of associational freedoms than the assessment of agency fees.

"In addition, [Abood] cited the risk of 'free riders' as justification for agency fees. [Petitioner] argues that he is not a free rider on a bus headed for a destination that he wishes to reach but is more like a person shanghaied for an unwanted voyage. [Avoiding] free riders is not a compelling interest. [Many] private groups speak out with the objective of obtaining government action that will have the effect of benefiting nonmembers. May all those who are thought to benefit from such efforts be compelled to subsidize this speech?

"[Those] supporting agency fees contend that the situation here is different because unions are statutorily required to represent the interests of all public employees in the unit, whether or not they are union members. Why might this matter? [It] is simply not true that unions will refuse to serve as the exclusive representative of all employees in the unit if they are not given agency fees. As noted, unions represent millions of public employees in jurisdictions that do not permit agency fees. No union is ever compelled to seek that designation. On the contrary, designation as exclusive representative is avidly sought.

"[There] remains the question whether *stare decisis* nonetheless counsels against overruling Abood. It does not. [*Stare decisis*] applies with perhaps least force of all to decisions that wrongly denied First Amendment rights. Our cases identify factors that should be taken into account in deciding whether to overrule a past decision. [An] important factor in determining whether a precedent should be overruled is the quality of its reasoning. [Abood] was poorly reasoned. [Abood] failed to appreciate the conceptual difficulty of distinguishing in public-sector cases between union expenditures that are made for collective-bargaining purposes and those that are made to achieve political ends. [Abood's] line between chargeable and nonchargeable union expenditures has proved to be impossible to draw with precision. [Objecting] employees also face a daunting and expensive task if they wish to challenge union chargeability determinations. [Developments] since Abood, both factual and legal, have also eroded the decision's underpinnings and left it an outlier among our First Amendment cases. Abood pinned its result on the unsupported empirical assumption that the principle of exclusive representation in the public sector is dependent on a union or agency shop. But [experience] has shown otherwise. It is also significant that the Court decided Abood against a very different legal and economic backdrop. Public-sector unionism was a relatively new phenomenon in 1977. [Since] then, public-sector union membership has come to surpass private-sector union membership, even though there are nearly four times as many total private-sector employees as public-sector employees. This ascendance of public-sector unions has been marked by a parallel increase in public spending. [Not] all that increase can be attributed to public-sector unions, of course, but the mounting costs of public-employee wages, benefits, and pensions undoubtedly played a substantial role. [Unsustainable] collective-bargaining agreements have also been blamed for multiple municipal bankruptcies. These developments, and the political debate over public spending and debt they have spurred, have given collective-bargaining issues a political valence that Abood did not fully appreciate. Abood is also an anomaly in our First Amendment jurisprudence [when] viewed against our cases holding that public employees generally may not be required to support a political party. [Reliance also] does not carry decisive weight. [It] would be unconscionable to permit free speech rights to be abridged in perpetuity in order to preserve contract provisions that will expire on their own in a few years' time. [Abood also] does not provide a clear or easily applicable standard, so arguments for reliance based on its clarity are misplaced. This is especially so because public-sector unions have been on notice for years regarding this Court's misgivings about Abood."

Justice KAGAN dissented, joined by Justices Ginsburg, Breyer, and Sotomayor: "For over 40 years, Abood struck a stable balance between public employees' First Amendment rights and government entities' interests in running their workforces as they thought proper. [The] Court's decisions have long made plain that government entities have substantial latitude to regulate their employees' speech—especially about terms of employment—in the interest of operating their workplaces effectively. [The] Abood regime was a paradigmatic example of how the government can regulate speech in its capacity as an employer. [The] decision will have large-scale consequences. Public employee unions will lose a secure source of financial support. State and local governments that thought fair-share provisions furthered their interests will need to find new ways of managing their workforces. Across the country, the relationships of public employees and employers will alter in both predictable and wholly unexpected ways. Rarely if ever has the Court overruled a decision [with] so little regard for the usual principles of *stare decisis*. [More] than 20 States have statutory schemes built on the decision. [Reliance] interests do not come any stronger. [And] likewise, judicial disruption does not get any greater.

"[The majority avoids] the key question, which is whether unions without agency fees will be *able to* (not whether they will *want to*) carry on as an effective exclusive representative. And as to that question, the majority again fails to reckon with how economically rational actors behave—in public as well as private workplaces. Without a fair-share agreement, the class of union non-members spirals upward. Employees (including those who love the union) realize that they can get the same benefits even if they let their memberships expire. And as more and more stop paying dues, those left must take up the financial slack (and anyway, begin to feel like suckers)—so they too quit the union. And when the vicious cycle finally ends, chances are that the union will lack the resources to effectively perform the responsibilities of an exclusive representative—or, in the worst case, to perform them at all. The result is to frustrate the interests of every government entity that thinks a strong exclusive-representation scheme will promote stable labor relations.

"In many cases over many decades, this Court has addressed how the First Amendment applies when the government, acting not as sovereign but as employer, limits its workers' speech. [It] must be able, much as a private employer is, to manage its workforce as it thinks fit. A public employee thus must submit to certain limitations on his or her freedom. Garcetti. [When] the government imposes speech restrictions relating to workplace operations, of the kind a private employer also would, the Court reliably upholds them. See, e.g., Connick. Like Pickering, Abood drew the constitutional line by analyzing the connection between the government's managerial interests and different kinds of expression.

"[But] the worse part of today's opinion is where the majority subverts all known principles of *stare decisis*. [Abood] is not just any precedent: It is embedded in the law (not to mention [in] the world) in a way not many decisions are. [Abood is not an outlier because it] coheres with the Pickering approach to reviewing regulation of public employees' speech. [The] majority is likewise wrong to invoke "workability" as a reason for overruling Abood. [As] exercises of constitutional linedrawing go, Abood stands well above average. In the 40 years since Abood, this Court has had to resolve only a handful of cases raising questions about the distinction.

"[One] *stare decisis* factor—reliance—dominates all others here. [The] Court today wreaks havoc on entrenched legislative and contractual arrangements. Over 20 States have by now enacted statutes authorizing fair-share provisions. [Thousands] of current contracts covering millions of workers provide for agency fees. [There] is no sugarcoating today's opinion. [The majority] prevents the American people [from] making important choices about workplace governance. And it does so by weaponizing the First Amendment, in a way that unleashes judges, now and in the future, to intervene in economic and regulatory policy.

"[The majority] has overruled Abood because it wanted to. Because, that is, it wanted to pick the winning side in what should be—and until now, has been—an energetic policy debate. [And] maybe most alarming, the majority has chosen the winners by turning the First Amendment into a sword, and using it against workaday economic and regulatory policy. [Speech] is everywhere—a part of every human activity (employment, health care, securities trading, you name it). For that reason, almost all economic and regulatory policy affects or touches speech. So the majority's road runs long. And at every stop are black-robed rulers overriding citizens' choices. The First Amendment was meant for better things."

SECTION 3. MONEY AND POLITICAL CAMPAIGNS

Page 1501. Add new Note after Note 4, *Are some contribution limits invalid?*

5.   ***Doctrinal reach of anticorruption rationale.*** In **McDonnell v. United States**, 579 U.S. ___, 136 S.Ct. 2355 (2016), the Court had to determine whether the former governor of Virginia had violated the Hobbs Act by taking gifts and cash in exchange for setting up meetings and hosting events. The Court held that McDonnell's actions did not count as "official acts" under the statute. It supported its holding in part on the basis of constitutional avoidance. Chief Justice ROBERTS wrote: "[T]he Government's expansive interpretation of 'official act' would raise significant constitutional concerns. Section 201 prohibits quid pro quo corruption—the exchange of a thing of value for an 'official act. In the Government's view, nearly anything a public official accepts—from a campaign contribution to lunch—counts as a quid; and nearly anything a public official does—from arranging a meeting to inviting a guest to an event—counts as a quo. But conscientious public officials arrange meetings for constituents, contact other officials on their behalf, and include them in events all the time. The basic compact underlying representative government assumes that public officials will hear from their constituents and act appropriately on their concerns—whether it is the union official worried about a plant closing or the homeowners who wonder why it took five days to restore power to their neighborhood after a storm. The Government's position could cast a pall of potential prosecution over these relationships if the union had given a campaign contribution in the past or the homeowners invited the official to join them on their annual outing to the ballgame. Officials might wonder whether they could respond to even the most commonplace requests for assistance, and citizens with legitimate concerns might shrink from participating in democratic discourse. [None] of this, of course, is to suggest that the facts of this case typify normal political interaction between public officials and their constituents. Far from it. But the Government's legal interpretation is not confined to cases involving extravagant gifts or large sums of money, and we cannot construe a criminal statute on the assumption that the Government will use it responsibly."

CHAPTER 14

THE RELIGION CLAUSES: FREE EXERCISE AND ESTABLISHMENT

SECTION 3. THE FREE EXERCISE OF RELIGION

Page 1570. Add new Note 4 after Note 3, *Religious or racial animosity?*

4. ***Expressions of bias and differential results.*** In **Masterpiece Cakeshop v. Colorado Civil Rights Commission**, 584 U.S. ___, 138 S.Ct. 1719 (2018), a Colorado baker told a same-sex couple that he would not create a cake for their wedding celebration because of his religious opposition to same-sex marriages. The couple filed a charge with the Colorado Civil Rights Commission pursuant to the Colorado Anti-Discrimination Act (CADA), which prohibits discrimination based on sexual orientation in a "place of business engaged in any sales to the public and any place offering services . . . to the public." The Colorado Civil Rights Division first found probable cause for a violation and referred the case to the Commission. The Commission then referred the case for a formal hearing before a state Administrative Law Judge (ALJ), who ruled in the couple's favor. The case received wide public attention as the first major post-Obergefell clash between religious liberty and marriage equality. Justice KENNEDY's opinion for a 7–2 Court ducked the major issues and instead found a Lukumi violation: "The freedoms asserted here are both the freedom of speech and the free exercise of religion. The free speech aspect of this case is difficult, for few persons who have seen a beautiful wedding cake might have thought of its creation as an exercise of protected speech. This is an instructive example, however, of the proposition that the application of constitutional freedoms in new contexts can deepen our understanding of their meaning. One of the difficulties in this case is that the parties disagree as to the extent of the baker's refusal to provide service. If a baker refused to design a special cake with words or images celebrating the marriage—for instance, a cake showing words with religious meaning—that might be different from a refusal to sell any cake at all. [The] same difficulties arise in determining whether a baker has a valid free exercise claim. A baker's refusal to attend the wedding to ensure that the cake is cut the right way, or a refusal to put certain religious words or decorations on the cake, or even a refusal to sell a cake that has been baked for the public generally but includes certain religious words or symbols on it are just three examples of possibilities that seem all but endless.

"[Our] society has come to the recognition that gay persons and gay couples cannot be treated as social outcasts or as inferior in dignity and worth. For that reason the laws and the Constitution can, and in some instances must, protect them in the exercise of their civil rights. The exercise of their freedom on terms equal to others must be given great weight and respect by the courts. At the same time, the religious and philosophical objections to gay marriage are protected views and in some instances protected forms of expression. [Nevertheless,] while those religious and philosophical objections are protected, it is a general rule that such objections do not allow business owners and other actors in the economy and in society to deny protected persons equal access to goods and services under a neutral and generally applicable public accommodations law. When it comes to weddings, it can be assumed that a member of the clergy who objects to gay marriage on moral and religious grounds could not be compelled to perform the ceremony without denial of his or her right to the free exercise of religion. This refusal would be well understood in our constitutional order as an exercise of religion, an exercise that gay persons could recognize and accept without serious diminishment to their own dignity and worth. Yet if that exception were not confined, then a long list of persons who provide goods and services for marriages and weddings might refuse to do so for gay persons, thus resulting in a community-wide stigma inconsistent with the history and dynamics of civil rights laws that ensure equal access to goods, services, and public accommodations.

"[The] neutral and respectful consideration to which Phillips was entitled was compromised here, however. The Civil Rights Commission's treatment of his case has some elements of a clear and impermissible hostility toward the sincere religious beliefs that motivated his objection. That hostility surfaced at the Commission's formal, public hearings, as shown by the record. [During the Commission's first public meeting,] commissioners endorsed the view that religious beliefs cannot legitimately be carried into the public sphere or commercial domain, implying that religious beliefs and persons are less than fully welcome in Colorado's business community. One commissioner suggested that Phillips can believe "what he wants to believe," but cannot act on his religious beliefs "if he decides to do business in the state." A few moments later, the commissioner restated the same position: "[I]f a businessman wants to do business in the state and he's got an issue with the—the law's impacting his personal belief system, he needs to look at being able to compromise." Standing alone, these statements are susceptible of different interpretations. On the one hand, they might mean simply that a business cannot refuse to provide services based on sexual orientation, regardless of the proprietor's personal views. On the other hand, they might be seen as inappropriate and dismissive comments showing lack of due consideration for Phillips' free exercise rights and the dilemma he faced. In view of the comments that followed, the latter seems the more likely.

"[At the Commission's second public meeting,] another commissioner made specific reference to the previous meeting's discussion but said far more to disparage Phillips' beliefs. The commissioner stated: ['Freedom] of religion and religion has been used to justify all kinds of discrimination throughout history, whether it be slavery, whether it be the holocaust, whether it be—I mean, we—we can list hundreds of situations where freedom of religion has been used to justify discrimination. And to me it is one of the most despicable pieces of rhetoric that people can use to—to use their religion to hurt others.' To describe a man's faith as 'one of the most despicable pieces of rhetoric that people can use' is to disparage his religion in at least two distinct ways: by describing it as despicable, and also by characterizing it as merely rhetorical—something insubstantial and even insincere. The commissioner even went so far as to compare Phillips' invocation of his sincerely held religious beliefs to defenses of slavery and the Holocaust. This sentiment is inappropriate for a Commission charged with the solemn responsibility of fair and neutral enforcement of Colorado's antidiscrimination law—a law that protects discrimination on the basis of religion as well as sexual orientation.

"The record shows no objection to these comments from other commissioners. And the later state-court ruling reviewing the Commission's decision did not mention those comments, much less express concern with their content. Nor were the comments by the commissioners disavowed in the briefs filed in this Court. For these reasons, the Court cannot avoid the conclusion that these statements cast doubt on the fairness and impartiality of the Commission's adjudication of Phillips' case. Members of the Court have disagreed on the question whether statements made by lawmakers may properly be taken into account in determining whether a law intentionally discriminates on the basis of religion. See Lukumi (Scalia, J., concurring in part and concurring in judgment). In this case, however, the remarks were made in a very different context—by an adjudicatory body deciding a particular case.

"Another indication of hostility is the difference in treatment between Phillips' case and the cases of other bakers who objected to a requested cake on the basis of conscience and prevailed before the Commission. [As] noted above, on at least three other occasions the Civil Rights Division considered the refusal of bakers to create cakes with images that conveyed disapproval of same-sex marriage, along with religious text. Each time, the Division found that the baker acted lawfully in refusing service. It made these determinations because, in the words of the Division, the requested cake included 'wording and images [the baker] deemed derogatory.' The treatment of the conscience-based objections at issue in these three cases contrasts with the Commission's treatment of Phillips' objection. The Commission ruled against Phillips in part on the theory that any message the requested wedding cake would carry would be attributed to the customer, not to the baker. Yet the Division did not address this point in any of the other cases with respect to the cakes depicting anti-gay marriage symbolism. Additionally, the Division found no violation of CADA in the other cases in part because each bakery was willing to sell other products, including those depicting Christian themes, to the prospective customers. But the Commission dismissed Phillips' willingness to sell 'birthday cakes, shower cakes, [and] cookies and brownies,' to gay and lesbian customers as irrelevant. The treatment of the other cases and Phillips' case could reasonably be interpreted as being inconsistent as to the question of whether speech is involved, quite apart from whether the cases should ultimately be distinguished."

Justice KAGAN concurred, joined by Justice Breyer: "I write separately to elaborate on one of the bases for the Court's holding. The Court partly relies on the disparate consideration of Phillips' case compared to the cases of [three] other bakers who objected to a requested cake on the basis of conscience. [What] makes the state agencies' consideration [disquieting] is that a proper basis for distinguishing the cases was available—in fact, was obvious. The Colorado Anti-Discrimination Act (CADA) makes it unlawful for a place of public accommodation to deny 'the full and equal enjoyment' of goods and services to individuals based on certain characteristics, including sexual orientation and creed. The three bakers in the cases [brought by William Jack] did not violate that law. Jack requested them to make a cake (one denigrating gay people and same-sex marriage) that they would not have made for any customer. In refusing that request, the bakers did not single out Jack because of his religion, but instead treated him in the same way they would have treated anyone else—just as CADA requires. By contrast, the same-sex couple in this case requested a wedding cake that Phillips would have made for an opposite-sex couple. In refusing that request, Phillips contravened CADA's demand that customers receive 'the full and equal enjoyment' of public accommodations irrespective of their sexual orientation. The different outcomes in the Jack cases and the Phillips case could thus have been justified by a plain reading and neutral application of Colorado law—untainted by any bias against a religious belief. I read the Court's opinion as fully consistent with that view."

Justice GORSUCH concurred, joined by Justice Alito, to disagree with Justice Kagan: "In both cases, the effect on the customer was the same: bakers refused service to persons who bore a statutorily protected trait (religious faith or sexual orientation). But in both cases the bakers refused service intending only to honor a personal conviction. To be sure, the bakers knew their conduct promised the effect of leaving a customer in a protected class unserved. But there's no indication the bakers actually intended to refuse service because of a customer's protected characteristic. We know this because all of the bakers explained without contradiction that they would not sell the requested cakes to anyone, while they would sell other cakes to members of the protected class (as well as to anyone else). So, for example, the bakers in the first case would have refused to sell a cake denigrating same-sex marriage to an atheist customer, just as the baker in the second case would have refused to sell a cake celebrating same-sex marriage to a heterosexual customer. And the bakers in the first case were generally happy to sell to persons of faith, just as the baker in the second case was generally happy to sell to gay persons. In both cases, it was the kind of cake, not the kind of customer, that mattered to the bakers.

"The distinction between intended and knowingly accepted effects is familiar in life and law. [The] problem here is that the Commission failed to act neutrally by applying a consistent legal rule. In Mr. Jack's case, the Commission chose to distinguish carefully between intended and knowingly accepted effects. [Yet,] in Mr. Phillips's case, the Commission dismissed this very same argument as resting on a 'distinction without a difference.' [The] Commission [cannot] slide up and down the mens rea scale, picking a mental state standard to suit its tastes depending on its sympathies."

Justice THOMAS, joined by Justice Gorsuch, concurred to say that the Court should have reached the free-speech issue because "creating and designing custom wedding cakes [is] expressive. Phillips considers himself an artist. [Phillips] is an active participant in the wedding celebration. He sits down with each couple for a consultation before he creates their custom wedding cake. [Wedding] cakes do, in fact, communicate [a] message. [Because] Phillips' conduct [was] expressive, Colorado's public-accommodations law cannot penalize it unless the law withstands strict scrutiny." He concluded: "In Obergefell, I warned that the Court's decision would inevitably come into conflict with religious liberty. [This] case proves that the conflict has already emerged."

Justice GINSBURG dissented, joined by Justice Sotomayor: "The different outcomes the Court features do not evidence hostility to religion of the kind we have previously held to signal a free-exercise violation, nor do the comments by one or two members of one of the four decisionmaking entities considering this case justify reversing the judgment below. [The] bakeries' refusal to make Jack cakes of a kind they would not make for any customer scarcely resembles Phillips' refusal to serve Craig and Mullins: Phillips would *not* sell to Craig and Mullins, for no reason other than their sexual orientation, a cake of the kind he regularly sold to others. When a couple contacts a bakery for a wedding cake, the product they are seeking is a cake celebrating *their* wedding—not a cake celebrating heterosexual weddings or same-sex weddings—and that is the service Craig and Mullins were denied. [Jack,] on the other hand, suffered no service refusal on the basis of his religion or any other protected characteristic. He was treated as any other customer would have been treated—no better, no worse.

"The fact that Phillips might sell other cakes and cookies to gay and lesbian customers was irrelevant to the issue Craig and Mullins' case presented. What matters is that Phillips would not provide a good or service to a same-sex couple that he would provide to a heterosexual couple. In contrast, the other bakeries' sale of other goods to Christian customers was relevant: It shows that there were no goods the bakeries would sell to a non-Christian customer that they would refuse to sell to a Christian customer.

"[Statements] made at the Commission's public hearings on Phillips' case provide no firmer support for the Court's holding today. [The] proceedings involved several layers of independent decisionmaking, of which the Commission was but one. [What] prejudice infected the determinations of the adjudicators in the case before and after the Commission? The Court does not say. Phillips' case is thus far removed from the only precedent upon which the Court relies, Lukumi, where the government action that violated a principle of religious neutrality implicated a sole decisionmaking body, the city council."

Does the Masterpiece Cakeshop decision break new ground in identifying antireligious animus? Were the commissioner's statements genuinely antireligious? The decision came out shortly before the decision in Trump v. Hawaii [Supplement p. 10], which declined to apply Lukumi analysis to President Donald Trump's allegedly anti-Muslim statements associated with his executive order banning travel from a several majority-Muslim countries. Is there tension between the two decisions?

SECTION 5. RECONCILING THE RELIGION CLAUSES

Page 1691. Add new Heading after the end of Note 2:

FUNDING FOR RELIGIOUS ENTITIES

Trinity Lutheran Church of Columbia, Inc. v. Comer

581 U.S. ___, 137 S.Ct. 2012, 198 L.Ed.2d 551 (2017).

■ ROBERTS, C. J., delivered the opinion of the Court, except as to footnote 3.

The Missouri Department of Natural Resources offers state grants to help public and private schools, nonprofit daycare centers, and other nonprofit entities purchase rubber playground surfaces made from recycled tires. Trinity Lutheran Church applied for such a grant for its preschool and daycare center and would have received one, but for the fact that Trinity Lutheran is a church. The Department had a policy [based on Article I, Section 7 of the Missouri Constitution] of categorically disqualifying churches and other religious organizations from receiving grants under its playground resurfacing program. The question presented is whether the Department's policy violated the rights of Trinity Lutheran under the Free Exercise Clause of the First Amendment.

II. [The] parties agree that the Establishment Clause [does] not prevent Missouri from including Trinity Lutheran in [its] Program. That does not, however, answer the question under the Free Exercise Clause, because we have recognized that there is "play in the joints" between what the Establishment Clause permits and the Free Exercise Clause compels.

III. A. [The] Department's policy expressly discriminates against otherwise eligible recipients by disqualifying them from a public benefit solely because of their religious character. [Such] a policy imposes a penalty on the free exercise of religion that triggers the most exacting scrutiny. [Like] the disqualification statute in McDaniel, the Department's policy puts Trinity Lutheran to a choice: It may participate in an otherwise available benefit program or remain a religious institution. Of course, Trinity Lutheran is free to continue operating as a church, just as McDaniel was free to continue being a minister. But that freedom comes at the cost of automatic and absolute exclusion from the benefits of a public program for which the Center is otherwise fully qualified. And when the State conditions a benefit in this way, [the] State has punished the free exercise of religion.

[It] is true the Department has not criminalized the way Trinity Lutheran worships or told the Church that it cannot subscribe to a certain view of the Gospel. But [as] the Court put it more than 50 years ago, "[i]t is too late in the day to doubt that the liberties of religion and expression may be infringed by the denial of or placing of conditions upon a benefit or privilege." Sherbert.

B.   [The] Department [argues] that the free exercise question in this case is instead controlled by our decision in Locke v. Davey. It is not. [Davey] was not denied a scholarship because of who he was; he was denied a scholarship because of what he proposed to do—use the funds to prepare for the ministry. Here there is no question that Trinity Lutheran was denied a grant simply because of what it is—a church.

The Court in Locke also stated that Washington's choice was in keeping with the State's antiestablishment interest in not using taxpayer funds to pay for the training of clergy; in fact, the Court could "think of few areas in which a State's antiestablishment interests come more into play." [Here] nothing of the sort can be said about a program to use recycled tires to resurface playgrounds.

[The] Department emphasizes Missouri's similar [tradition] of not furnishing taxpayer money directly to churches. But Locke took account of Washington's antiestablishment interest only after determining [that] the scholarship program did not "require students to choose between their religious beliefs and receiving a government benefit." [In] this case, there is no dispute that Trinity Lutheran is put to the choice between being a church and receiving a government benefit. The rule is simple: No churches need apply.[2]

C.   Under [the "most rigorous scrutiny] standard, only a state interest "of the highest order" can justify the Department's discriminatory policy. Yet the Department offers nothing more than Missouri's policy preference for skating as far as possible from religious establishment concerns. In the face of the clear infringement on free exercise before us, that interest cannot qualify as compelling.

■ JUSTICE THOMAS, with whom JUSTICE GORSUCH joins, concurring in part.

[This] Court's endorsement in Locke of even a "mild kind" of discrimination against religion remains troubling. But because the Court today appropriately construes Locke narrowly, see Part III-B, ante, and because no party has asked us to reconsider it, I join nearly all of the Court's opinion.

■ JUSTICE GORSUCH, with whom JUSTICE THOMAS joins, concurring in part.

[I] offer only two modest qualifications.

First, the Court leaves open the possibility a useful distinction might be drawn between laws that discriminate on the basis of religious status and religious use. Respectfully, I harbor doubts about the stability of such a line. Does a religious man say grace before dinner? Or does a man begin his meal in a religious manner? Is it a religious group that built the playground? Or did a group build the playground so it might be used to advance a religious mission? The distinction blurs in much the same way the line between acts

---

[2]   [Footnote 3 to the opinion of the Court]: This case involves express discrimination based on religious identity with respect to playground resurfacing. We do not address religious uses of funding or other forms of discrimination.

and omissions can blur when stared at too long, leaving us to ask (for example) whether the man who drowns by awaiting the incoming tide does so by act (coming upon the sea) or omission (allowing the sea to come upon him).

[Second] and for similar reasons, I am unable to join the footnoted observation, n. 3, that "[t]his case involves express discrimination based on religious identity with respect to playground resurfacing." Of course the footnote is entirely correct, but I worry that some might mistakenly read it to suggest that only "playground resurfacing" cases, or only those with some association with children's safety or health, or perhaps some other social good we find sufficiently worthy, are governed by the legal rules recounted in and faithfully applied by the Court's opinion. [And] the general principles here do not permit discrimination against religious exercise—whether on the playground or anywhere else.

■ Justice Breyer, concurring in the judgment.

[I] find relevant, and would emphasize, the particular nature of the "public benefit" here at issue. The Court stated in Everson that "cutting off church schools from" such "general government services as ordinary police and fire protection . . . is obviously not the purpose of the First Amendment." Here, the State would cut Trinity Lutheran off from participation in a general program designed to secure or to improve the health and safety of children. I see no significant difference. [I] would leave the application of the Free Exercise Clause to other kinds of public benefits for another day.

■ Justice Sotomayor, with whom Justice Ginsburg joins, dissenting.

[This] case is about nothing less than the relationship between religious institutions and the civil government—that is, between church and state. The Court today profoundly changes that relationship by holding, for the first time, that the Constitution requires the government to provide public funds directly to a church. Its decision slights both our precedents and our history, and its reasoning weakens this country's longstanding commitment to a separation of church and state beneficial to both.

[This] is a case about whether Missouri can decline to fund improvements to the facilities the Church uses to practice and spread its religious views. [The] Court has repeatedly warned that [payments] from the government to a house of worship would cross the line drawn by the Establishment Clause. [The] Establishment Clause does not allow Missouri to grant the Church's funding request because the Church uses the Learning Center, including its playground, in conjunction with its religious mission.

[The] Court may simply disagree with this account of the facts and think that the Church does not put its playground to religious use. If so, its mistake is limited to this case. But if it agrees that the State's funding would further religious activity and sees no Establishment Clause problem, then it must be implicitly applying a rule other than the one agreed to in our precedents. [Such] a break with precedent would mark a radical mistake.

[Even] assuming the absence of an Establishment Clause violation and proceeding on the Court's preferred front—the Free Exercise Clause—the Court errs. It claims that the government may not draw lines based on an entity's religious "status." But we have repeatedly said that it can. [The] play in the joints between the Free Exercise and Establishment Clauses gives government some room to recognize the unique status of religious entities and to single them out on that basis for exclusion from otherwise generally applicable laws.

[The] State need not, for example, fund the training of a religious group's leaders, those "who will preach their beliefs, teach their faith, and carry out their mission." It may instead avoid the historic "antiestablishment interests" raised by the use of "taxpayer funds to support church leaders." Locke.

Missouri has decided that the unique status of houses of worship requires a special rule when it comes to public funds. [Missouri's] decision, which has deep roots in our Nation's history, reflects a reasonable and constitutional judgment. [The] use of public funds to support core religious institutions can safely be described as a hallmark of the States' early experiences with religious establishment. Every state establishment saw laws passed to raise public funds and direct them toward houses of worship and ministers. And as the States all disestablished, one by one, they all undid those laws. [In] Locke, this Court expressed an understanding of, and respect for, this history.

[Like] the use of public dollars for ministers at issue in Locke, turning over public funds to houses of worship implicates serious anti-establishment and free exercise interests. [As] was true in Locke, a prophylactic rule against the use of public funds for houses of worship is a permissible accommodation of these weighty interests. The rule has a historical pedigree identical to that of the provision in Locke. Almost all of the States that ratified the Religion Clauses operated under this rule. Seven had placed this rule in their State Constitutions. Three enforced it by statute or in practice. Only one had not yet embraced the rule. Today, thirty-eight States have a counterpart to Missouri's Article I, § 7.10 The provisions, as a general matter, date back to or before these States' original Constitutions. That so many States have for so long drawn a line that prohibits public funding for houses of worship, based on principles rooted in this Nation's understanding of how best to foster religious liberty, supports the conclusion that public funding of houses of worship "is of a different ilk." Locke.

[The Court also] suggests that this case is different because it involves "discrimination" in the form of the denial of access to a possible benefit. But in this area of law, a decision to treat entities differently based on distinctions that the Religion Clauses make relevant does not amount to discrimination.

At bottom, the Court creates the following rule today: The government may draw lines on the basis of religious status to grant a benefit to religious persons or entities but it may not draw lines on that basis when doing so would further the interests the Religion Clauses protect in other ways. Nothing supports this lopsided outcome.